SCIENCE JOURNAL

McGRAW-HILL
SCIENCE

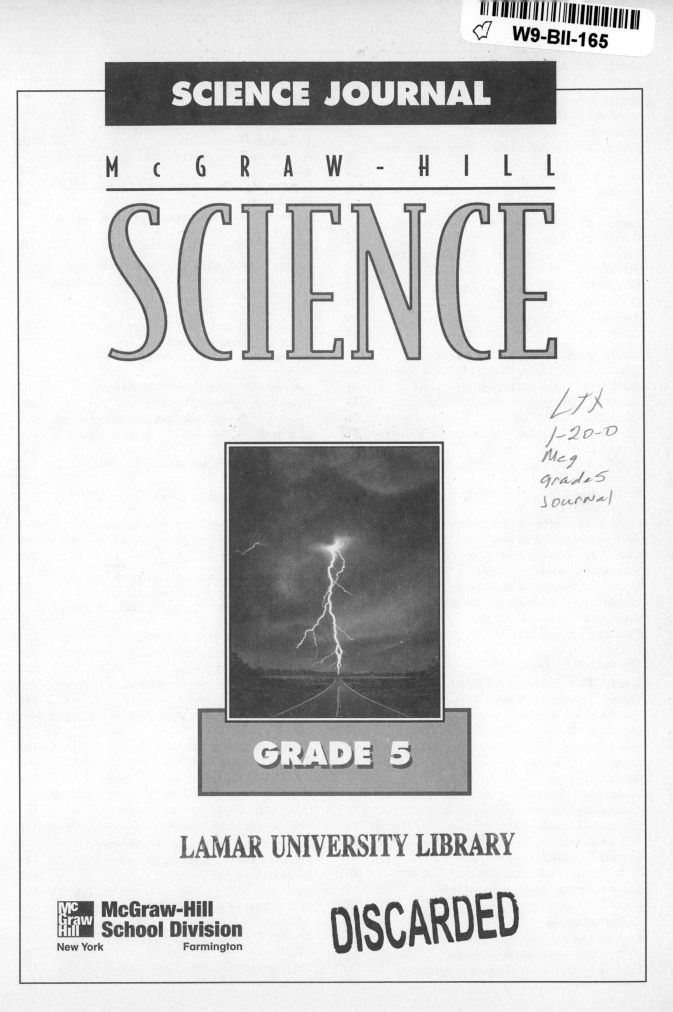

GRADE 5

LAMAR UNIVERSITY LIBRARY

Table of Contents

Investigate Where Plants Get Their Mass

Hypothesize Where do plants get their mass?

Write a **Hypothesis:**

_____

_____

Where do you think the extra mass comes from as a plant grows? Test your ideas.

Materials

- package of lima bean seeds
- soil
- water
- 4 paper cups
- balance
- ruler

Procedures

1. Fill the paper cups with a premeasured amount of soil. Use the same amount for each cup. Record the mass of the soil and the date.

   _____

2. Find the mass of the seed. Record it and the date. Plant one lima bean seed in each cup.

   _____

3. Place the cups where they will get sunlight. Water the soil the same amount each week.

4. **Observe** After three months, measure the plant height with the ruler and record your findings.

   _____

   Carefully remove the plant and root from the soil. Find the mass of the plant, and record it.

   _____

   Find the mass of the soil again, and record it.

   _____

5. **Interpret Data** Compare the mass of the plant and soil now to the start of the experiment. _____

   _____

SAMPLE DATA		
	September	**December**
Plant height	7.6 cm (3 in.)	25.4 cm (10 in.)
Mass of plant	2 g	68 g
Mass of soil	225 g	223 g

Conclude and Apply

1. Draw Conclusions How much mass did the plant gain in three months?

_____

2. Do you think the added mass of the plant came from the soil? Why? Do you think it came from the water you added? Explain.

_____

_____

_____

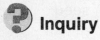 **Inquiry**

Think of your own questions that you might test.

My Question Is:

_____

How I Can Test It:

_____

_____

My Results Are:

_____

_____

Investigate What Plants Have in Common

Hypothesize Most plants live on land, but some live in water. Some are tiny, and others grow very large. Do all plants have common traits?

Write a **Hypothesis:**

_____

_____

Define what a plant is by observing four plants and comparing their characteristics.

Materials

- *Elodea* plant
- coverslip
- geranium (or other flowering plant)
- moss plant
- microscope
- dropper
- fern plant
- microscope slide
- water

Procedures

1. **Observe** Your group will need to get four plants from your teacher. Observe each of the plants.

2. **Communicate** As you observe each plant, draw the plant on a separate piece of paper. Describe each plant.

   _____

   _____

   _____

3. Make a wet-mount slide of an *Elodea* leaf by placing the leaf in a drop of water in the center of the slide and carefully putting a coverslip on top.

4. **Observe** View the slide under low power.

   _____

5. **Communicate** In the space below, draw what you see under low power.

Conclude and Apply

1. Communicate What plant traits can you observe without using the microscope?

_____

_____

2. Communicate What other plant traits can you observe with the microscope?

_____

_____

3. Define Based on what you observed, come up with your own definition of a plant.

_____

_____

Going Further: Problem Solving

4. Hypothesize Examine some other kinds of plants with the microscope.
Do all the plants seem to have the same traits, or do some plants look quite
different from the others? Do plants that look similar under the microscope
have the same traits? How would you set up an experiment to find out?

_____

_____

_____

 Inquiry

Think of your own questions that you might like to test. What traits are common in
plant cells?

My Question Is:

_____

How I Can Test It:

_____

My Results Are:

_____

_____

Tube-like Plant Parts

Hypothesize How does water get to different parts of a plant?

Write a **Hypothesis:**

_____

_____

Materials

- celery stalk
- oak or maple leaf
- hand lens

- bit of moss
- water
- knife

- lettuce leaf
- food coloring
- narrow-mouthed bottle

Procedures

1. **Observe/Communicate** Use the hand lens to examine the plant parts. Describe the structures you see.

_____

_____

_____

2. **Hypothesize** Make a guess about the function of each structure.

_____

_____

_____

_____

3. Add water to the bottle so the water is about an inch deep. Add a few drops of food coloring to the water.

4. Try putting different plant pieces in the colored water. Observe them after a few minutes. Record your observations.

_____

_____

Conclude and Apply

1. **Interpret Data** Write an explanation. Include a statement about why your observations support or don't support your guess.

_____

_____

_____

_____

_____

_____

_____

Going Further The tube-like structure, or vascular tissue, in a celery stem transports water very well. How can you demonstrate water moving up a tube? Write ad conduct an experiment.

My Hypothesis Is:

_____

_____

My Experiment Is:

_____

_____

_____

My Results Are:

_____

_____

Investigate How a Plant's Parts Help It Survive

Hypothesize How may plants from different places differ from each other? How do the differences help the plants survive in their surroundings?

Write a **Hypothesis:**

_____

_____

_____

Observe differences in plants that come from different environments.

Materials

- cactus
- water plant, such as an *Elodea* or a duckweed
- flowering plant, such as a geranium

Procedures

1. **Observe** Look at the physical properties of the leaves of each plant. Note the color, size, and shape of the leaves.

   _____

   _____

2. **Analyze** List any other plant parts that you see.

   _____

   _____

3. **Communicate** Observe the physical properties of these parts and record your observations.

   _____

   _____

4. Record any other physical properties that you observe.

   _____

   _____

Conclude and Apply

1. **Draw Conclusions** How do the parts of a cactus help it survive in a hot, dry desert?

_____

_____

2. **Infer** Would the geranium be able to survive in the desert? Why or why not?

_____

_____

3. **Infer** Could the water plant survive out of water? Why or why not?

_____

Going Further: Problem Solving

4. **Predict** Could these plants survive outdoors where you live? Why or why not? For each plant what conditions would you have to change so that the plant could survive outside where you live?

_____

_____

_____

Inquiry

Think of your own questions that you might like to test. How do plants adapt to the change of seasons?

My Question Is:

_____

How I Can Find Out:

_____

_____

My Results Are:

_____

Leaves

Hypothesize In what ways are the leaves that are important to you alike?
In what ways are they different?

Write a **Hypothesis:**

_____

_____

_____

Materials

• various plant leaves that you eat
• hand lens

Procedures

1. Collect a variety of different leaves that you eat as food.

2. **Observe** Examine them with a hand lens. Record your observations.

_____

_____

_____

3. **Compare** What do the leaves you brought have in common?

_____

4. **Compare** In what ways are they different from each other?

_____

_____

Conclude and Apply

1. **Communicate** Write how the leaves you examined are similar and how they
   are different.

_____

_____

2. Compare and Contrast Compare the leaves you examined with the leaves
your classmates looked at. In what ways are your leaves similar to theirs? In
what ways are they different?

_____

_____

Going Further What parts of plants are vegetables? What parts of plants do people
eat? Write and conduct an experiment.

My Hypothesis Is:

_____

_____

My Experiment Is:

_____

_____

My Results Are:

_____

_____

_____

_____

_____

_____

Root	Stem	Bud	Fruit	Seed

Investigate What Light Does for a Plant

Hypothesize How will a plant change if it does not get sunlight for several days? Why does it change?

Write a **Hypothesis:**

_____

_____

Observe how plant leaves are affected when they don't get light.

Materials

- growing plant (window plants from home or plants from an aquarium)
- opaque paper or aluminum foil

Safety Be sure to wash your hands after handling the plants.

Procedures

1. Cover part of a leaf of a growing plant.

2. **Using Variables** Cover a least four different leaves of the plant in the same way.

3. Place the whole plant in a window that gets lots of light.

4. **Collect Data** Remove the foil from one leaf after one class period. How is that leaf different from the uncovered leaves? Record your observations. Then cover the leaf again.

_____

_____

5. **Collect Data** Continue your observations. Remove the foil from another leaf after one day, another after two days, and another after a week. Record your observations. Replace the foil each time.

_____

_____

Conclude and Apply

1. **Observe** After one class period, how was the leaf you had just uncovered different from the uncovered leaves?

_____

_____

2. Identify Patterns How did the difference you noticed change after a day, two days, and a week?

_____

_____

3. Draw Conclusions How do light and darkness affect the growth of leaves?

_____

_____

Going Further: Problem Solving

4. Use Variables Remove the coverings from the four leaves and observe them for another week. How do they respond to being uncovered? Do their differences from the other leaves remain or disappear?

_____

_____

_____

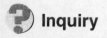 **Inquiry**

Think of your own questions that you might test. What are the best levels of light for geraniums and impatiens?

My Question Is:

_____

_____

How I Can Test It:

_____

_____

_____

My Results Are:

_____

_____

Experimenting

Why Do Leaves Change Color?

To find an answer to this question, the first thing you might do is figure out what changes occur in the fall that *might* cause leaves to change color. Scientists call such changes *variables*. You might identify two of these variables as the amount of daylight and the temperature, both of which go down in the fall.

Next you would make a guess that *seems* to make sense about which variable causes leaves to change color. This guess is called a *hypothesis*. It is often made in the form of an *if . . . then . . .* statement. For example, "*If* the plant doesn't get water, *then* it won't grow." To see if your hypothesis is a good idea, you would perform an experiment. That experiment has to be set up so that it gives a clear answer.

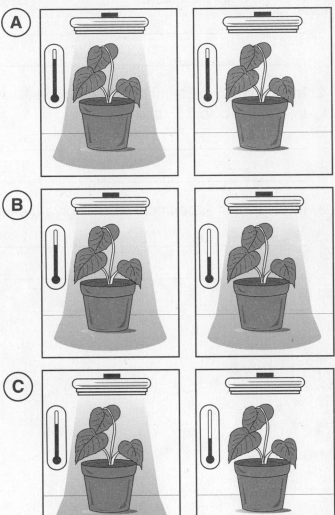

Procedures

1. Look at the drawings. They show three experiments—A, B, C. Study the setups.

2. **Observe** What variable or variables are being tested in the first experiment? Write your answer. What variable or variables are being tested in the other two experiments.

_____

_____

Conclude and Apply

1. Infer Which experiment is testing to see whether light causes leaves to change color? Explain.

_____

_____

2. Infer Which experiment is testing to see whether temperature causes leaves to change color? Explain why.

_____

_____

3. Infer Which experiment will not give a clear answer? Explain why not.

_____

_____

Investigate How Mosses Get Water

Hypothesize Why do ferns grow tall while mosses grow only very close to the ground? How do the parts of mosses help them live where they do?

Write a **Hypothesis:**

_____

_____

_____

_____

_____

Examine a moss plant to find out how its parts allow the plant to live where it does.

Materials

- hand lens
- 3 microscope slides
- moss plant
- forceps
- coverslip
- dropper
- microscope

Procedures

1. **Observe** Place a moss on a paper towel. Examine it with a hand lens. Find its rootlike parts. Use the hand lens to view the stemlike and leaflike parts. Record your observations.

_____

_____

2. **Measure** Use the forceps to remove a leaflike part. Make a wet-mount slide of the part. Observe its cells using the microscope on low power. Determine how thick the leaflike part is by moving the focus up and down.

3. **Observe** Find a capsule-shaped object at the end of the brownish stalk. Observe it with the hand lens. Place the capsule on a slide. Add a drop of water. Place a second slide on top of the capsule. Press down on the top slide with your thumb and crush the capsule. Carefully remove the top slide and place a coverslip over the crushed capsule.

4. **Observe** Examine the released structures under low power. On a separate sheet of paper, draw what you see.

Conclude and Apply

1. Observe Which parts of the moss are green? Explain why they are green.

_____

_____

2. Observe How many cell layers make up the leaflike structure?

_____

3. Interpret Data What structures anchor the moss plant? What was
the capsule?

_____

_____

Going Further: Problem Solving

4. Predict What do you think the objects inside the capsule do? How would
you set up an experiment to test your prediction?

_____

_____

_____

Inquiry

Think of your own questions that you might like to test. How do cells of mosses
compare with other plants.

My Question Is:

_____

_____

How I Can Test It:

_____

_____

My Results Are:

_____

_____

Ferns

Hypothesize In what ways are ferns and mosses alike and different?
Examine a fern and compare the results to those from the Explore Activity.

Write a **Hypothesis:**

_____

_____

Materials

- fern plant
- microscope
- toothpick

- fern leaf with spore cases
- microscope slide
- water

Procedures

1. **Observe** Carefully examine the whole fern plant. Look at the stem.
   Observe how the leaves grow from the stem. Find veins in the leaves.
   Record your observations.

   _____

   _____

2. **Observe** Find a leaf whose bottom is covered with brownish spots. These
   are spore cases.

3. **Experiment** Place a drop of water on a clean slide. Use a toothpick to
   scrape one of the spore cases into the drop of water. Observe the spore
   case under the low power of a microscope.

Conclude and Apply

1. **Observe** What do the spore cases contain?

_____

2. **Infer** What do fern and mosses have in common?

_____

_____

Going Further What is the function of fern spores? How can you demonstrate this? Write and conduct an experiment.

My Hypothesis Is:

_____

_____

My Experiment Is:

_____

_____

My Results Are:

_____

_____

Investigate How Seed Plants Differ

Hypothesize Have you ever noticed the differences in plant leaves? Are some leaves larger than others? How do these differences help the plant survive?

Write a **Hypothesis:**

_____

_____

Compare the leaves of three kinds of plants to find how they enable each plant to survive in its environment.

Materials

- microscope
- coverslip
- hand lens
- microscope slide
- grass plant
- small pine seedling or other conifer
- garden plant or house plant, such as geranium

Procedures

1. **Observe** Examine each plant. Use the hand lens to examine a leaf from each one. On a separate piece of paper, draw each leaf and label it with the name of the plant it came from.

2. **Observe** Remove a part of the lower epidermis from the grass leaf. Make a wet-mount slide. Examine the slide under low power.

3. **Communicate** On a separate piece of paper, draw what you observe.

4. **Observe** Repeat step 2 with a pine needle and a houseplant leaf (such as a geranium). On a separate piece of paper, draw what you observe.

Conclude and Apply

1. **Compare and Contrast** How are the leaves of the three plants alike? How are the leaves of the three plants different from one another?

_____

_____

_____

_____

_____

2. Infer Which one of the plants do you think is least like the other two?
Explain your reasoning.

_____

_____

Going Further: Problem Solving

3. Experiment Predict which of the plants you examined could survive best in
a dry environment. How do you think the plant's leaves would help it do this?
Design an experiment that would test your prediction.

_____

_____

_____

_____

 Inquiry

Think of your own questions that you might like to test. How are stomata related
to water loss in the leaf?

My Question Is:

_____

_____

How I Can Test It:

_____

_____

_____

_____

My Results Are:

_____

_____

_____

Name

Classifying

Flowering Plants

In this activity you will classify flowering plants. That is, you will examine several plants and try to determine whether each is a monocot or a dicot. As you examine each plant sample, refer to the chart of Main Differences Between Monocots and Dicots to help you classify each sample.

Materials

• sample leaves and flowers from various angiosperms

Procedures

1. **Observe** Get together with a few of your classmates and go on a leaf-and flower-collecting field trip. (Make sure to avoid poison ivy, poison oak, and poison sumac leaves. Your teacher can tell you how to spot them.)

2. **Observe** Find a number of different angiosperms. Try to get a sample of a leaf and flower from each plant. If you can't get a flower, a leaf will do.

3. **Interpret Data** Look at the chart of Main Differences Between Monocots and Dicots. It will give you clues on how to tell if the sample leaves and flowers you chose are monocots or dicots.

Main Differences Between Monocots and Dicots		
Characteristics	**Monocots**	**Dicots**
Cotyledons	One	Two
Leaf veins	Parallel	Branched
Flower parts	Multiples of three	Multiples of four or five
Vascular system	In bundles	Scattered in rings

Conclude and Apply

1. **Observe** Examine the plant parts you have chosen. For each sample leaf, describe how the leaf veins look. For each sample flower, tell how many parts each flower has. Record your answers in the chart.

Plant Name	Venation (parallel or branched)	Number of Flower Parts (multiple of 3, 4, or 5)	Monocot or Dicot

2. **Classify** Mount the leaves and flowers on a heavy sheet of cardboard, and indicate in the above chart whether each came from a monocot or a dicot.

Design Your Own Experiment

How Do Flowers Differ?

Hypothesize Are all flowers alike? If not, how are flowers different? How are they alike? What do you think plants use their flowers for?

Write a **Hypothesis:**

_____

_____

Materials

- several large flowers from different plants
- forceps
- toothpick

- hand lens
- dropper
- black paper

Procedures

1. **Plan** Decide on how you will compare the flowers you look at. You may choose to look for parts that they seem to have in common. Describe what the parts are and how they differ from plant to plant.

_____

_____

_____

_____

_____

2. Begin by removing the outer leaflike parts. Examine them. On a separate sheet of paper, draw what they look like.

3. Remove the petals. Examine them. Draw what they look like on a separate piece of paper.

4. **Observe** Examine the rest of the flowers as you decide.

5. **Communicate** On a separate piece of paper, draw the parts you examined.

Conclude and Apply

1. **Communicate** What color is each flower? What do you think the job of the petals is? How would you design an experiment to find out?

   _____

   _____

2. **Infer** What do you think the various parts of each flower are for? Do you think the same parts of different types of flowers do the same kinds of jobs for their plants?

   _____

   _____

Going Further: Apply

3. **Infer** Why do you think a plant has flowers? Make a hypothesis. Design an experiment to test your ideas.

   _____

   _____

   _____

Inquiry

Think of your own questions that you might like to test. How do the inner parts help the plant to reproduce?

My Question Is:

_____

How I Can Test It:

_____

_____

My Results Are:

_____

Inside a Seed

Hypothesize What does a seed do? Where does it store its food? How do different seeds compare?

Write a **Hypothesis:**

_____

_____

_____

_____

Materials

- bean seed (such as a lima bean)
- water
- corn seed
- hand lens

Procedures

1. Soak the bean seed in water overnight.

2. **Observe** Then carefully pull apart the two halves of the seed. Examine the halves with a hand lens.

3. **Communicate** Draw what you see.

Conclude and Apply

1. **Infer** Which part of the seed is the embryo?

   _____

   _____

2. **Identify** On your drawing, label the seed coat and the place where you think food is stored.

   _____

   _____

3. **Compare and Contrast** Look at a corn seed. Describe how its parts are similar to or different from a bean seed.

   _____

   _____

   _____

4. **Communicate** Explain why you think one is the seed of a dicot and the other is the seed of a monocot. Which is which?

   _____

   _____

Going Further What type of vein structure would you expect for corn and bean leaves? How can you verify your answer? Write and conduct an experiment.

My Hypothesis Is:

_____

_____

My Experiment Is:

_____

My Results Are:

_____

_____

Investigate How Roots Grow

Hypothesize Do roots always grow "down" no matter how you plant a seed?

Write a **Hypothesis:**

_____

Place seeds in many positions to observe how roots grow from them.

Materials

- petri dish (plastic)
- marking pen
- 2 paper towels
- tape
- 4 bean seeds that have been soaked in water overnight

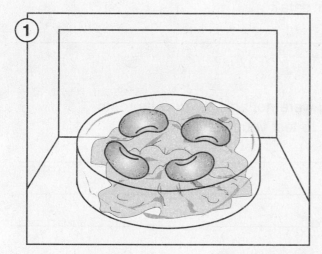
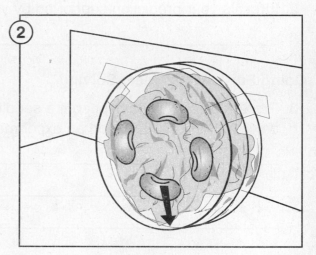

Procedures

1. Soak two paper towels. Wrinkle the paper towels and place them in the bottom half of the petri dish.

2. Place the four seeds on top of the wet paper towels as shown in diagram 1. Place the seeds so the curved part is turned toward the center of the dish.

3. Place the top on the petri dish. The top will hold the seeds in the wet paper towels. Seal the top with transparent tape. Draw an arrow on the petri dish with the glass-marking pen as shown in diagram 2. This will show which direction is down. Write the number or name of your group on the petri dish.

4. In a place your teacher provides, stand the petri dish on its edge so the arrow is pointing downward. Tape the petri dish so that it will remain standing. Do not lay the dish down flat.

5. **Predict** Make a prediction about the direction you think the roots will grow.

_____

6. Communicate Examine the seeds for the next four days. Record the direction of root growth.

_____

_____

Conclude and Apply

1. Observe In what direction were the roots growing on day 1? On day 4?

_____

_____

2. Infer Is your prediction supported by your data?

_____

Going Further: Problem Solving

3. Predict What would happen if a seedling were not able to grow its roots down into the soil? Design an experiment to test your prediction.

_____

_____

_____

Inquiry

Think of your own questions that you might like to test. What happens if a germinated seed is disturbed so that the orientation of the roots is changed?

My Question Is:

_____

_____

How I Can Test It:

_____

_____

My Results Are:

_____

Plants Compete for Light

Hypothesize Do some plants need more light than others? Can some plants survive in shady areas?

Write a **Hypothesis:**

_____

_____

Materials

- grass seed
- various houseplants
- soil
- ivy plant
- paper cup

Procedures

1. Collect samples of various house plants that grow to different widths and heights.

2. Plant them, with some grass seed, in your cup. Record the types of plants you used.

_____

3. **Observe** Examine your plants over the next few days.

Conclude and Apply

1. **Observe** Which are being shaded by others? Are the plants in the shade doing as well as the plants that are getting more light?

_____

_____

2. **Hypothesize** How would you design an experiment to test which plants need more light to grow? How could you determine if these plants have anything else in common?

_____

_____

_____

_____

Going Further The previous experiment demonstrated that plants require different intensities of light to thrive. Are plants also sensitive to the amount of time they are exposed to light? Write and conduct an experiment.

My Hypothesis Is:

_____

_____

My Experiment Is:

_____

_____

_____

_____

_____

_____

My Results Are:

_____

_____

_____

_____

Investigate If the Sun's Angle Matters

Hypothesize How does the angle at which the Sun's energy hits Earth affect the warming of Earth?

Write a **Hypothesis:**

_____

_____

Test what factors might affect how warm an area gets.

Materials

- 3 thermometers
- triangular blocks
- black paper
- white paper

- centimeter ruler
- scissors
- tape
- 150-W clear bulb lamp

- stopwatch
- foam bowl
- clay

Procedures

Safety Do not look into the lamplight. Prop up a foam bowl, using a plate or clay, to shield your eyes from the light.

1. Place a thermometer onto each of the three blocks, as shown. Cover each with black paper. Put blocks 20 cm from the bulb, level with its filament (curly wire).

2. **Observe** Measure the starting temperature at each block. Record the temperatures.

_____

3. **Predict** What will happen when the lamp is turned on? Turn the lamp on. Record the temperature at each block every two minutes, for ten minutes, in a data table on another sheet of paper.

_____

_____

4. Communicate On another sheet of paper, make a line graph showing the change in temperature at each block over time.

5. Use Variables Repeat the activity with white paper.

Conclude and Apply

1. Communicate Which block's surface was warmed most by the lamplight? Which block's surface was warmed the least?

_____

_____

2. Infer How does the angle at which light hits a surface affect how much the surface is heated? How does the surface color affect how much it is heated?

_____

_____

_____

Going Further: Problem Solving

3. Experiment What other factors might affect how much a surface is warmed by sunlight? How would you test your ideas?

_____

_____

_____

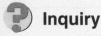 **Inquiry**

Think of your own questions that you might like to test. What other factors might affect temperature?

My Question Is:

_____

How I Can Test It:

_____

My Results Are:

_____

Investigating Angles

Hypothesize Why does the angle of insolation cause a difference in warming?

Write a **Hypothesis:**

_____

_____

_____

_____

Materials

- flashlight
- sheet of graph paper
- modeling clay
- ruler
- 3 toothpicks

Procedures

1. Fold a sheet of graph paper lengthwise in three equal parts. Put a small lump of clay in the middle of each part. Stand a toothpick straight up in each lump of clay.

2. Hold a flashlight directly over the first toothpick. Have a partner trace a line around the circle of light and trace the toothpick shadow.

3. **Use Variables** Repeat step 2 for the other two toothpicks, changing only the angle of the flashlight.

4. **Measure** Count the number of boxes in each circle. Measure the lengths of the toothpick shadows. Record your results.

Toothpick	Number of Boxes	Length of Shadow
1		
2		
3		

Conclude and Apply

1. Infer How is the length of the shadows related to the angle?

_____

_____

2. Infer How is the number of boxes in the circle related to the angle?

_____

_____

Going Further How does the angle of insolation affect where you live? Compare and contrast the local climate with the climate at the equator and at Earth's poles. Write and conduct an experiment.

My Hypothesis Is:

_____

_____

_____

My Experiment Is:

_____

_____

_____

_____

My Results Are:

_____

_____

_____

_____

Design Your Own Experiment

Where Does the Puddle Come From?

Hypothesize The lemonade glass on page 110 in your textbook has moisture on the side and in a puddle around the bottom. Where does the moisture come from? Is it from inside the glass? Write a hypothesis. How might you design an experiment to test your ideas?

Write a **Hypothesis:**

_____

_____

_____

Materials

- plastic drinking glasses
- paper towels
- ice
- food coloring
- thermometer
- goggles

Procedures 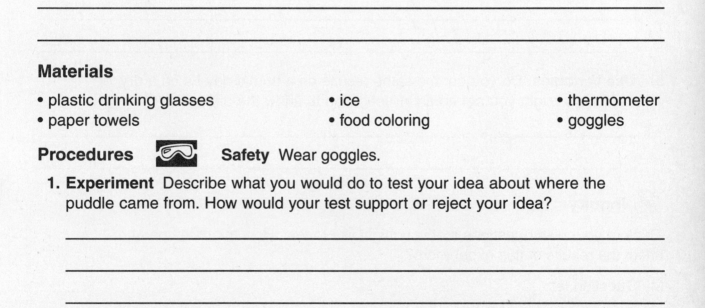 **Safety** Wear goggles.

1. **Experiment** Describe what you would do to test your idea about where the puddle came from. How would your test support or reject your idea?

    _____

    _____

    _____

    _____

2. **Communicate** On another sheet of paper draw a diagram showing how you would use the materials. Keep a record of your observations.

Conclude and Apply

1. **Communicate** Describe the results of your investigation.

    _____

    _____

2. **Communicate** What evidence did you gather? Explain what happened.

    _____

    _____

3. Infer How does this evidence support or reject your explanation?

_____

_____

Going Further: Problem Solving

4. Use Variables Do you get the same results on a cool day as on a warm day? How might you set up an investigation to show the difference?

_____

_____

_____

_____

5. Use Variables Do you get the same results on a humid day as on a dry day? How might you set up an investigation to show the difference?

_____

_____

 Inquiry

Think of your own questions that you might like to test. How might temperature affect the results of this experiment?

My Question Is:

_____

_____

How I Can Test It:

_____

_____

My Results Are:

_____

_____

Transpiration

Hypothesize What evidence can you find for transpiration?

Write a **Hypothesis:**

_____

_____

Materials

- potted houseplant (geraniums work well)
- transparent plastic bag

Procedures

1. Place the plastic bag completely over the plant, and secure it tightly around the base of the stem. Do not put the soil-filled pot into the bag.

2. **Observe** Place the plant in a sunny location, and observe it several times a day. Record your observations.

_____

_____

3. When you are done, remove the plastic bag from the plant.

Conclude and Apply

1. **Communicate** Describe what you see on the inside of the bag. Explain what happened.

_____

_____

_____

2. **Draw Conclusions** *Transpiration* sounds like *perspiration*—sweating. How might the two processes be alike?

_____

_____

3. **Predict** How would your results vary if you put the plant in the shade?

_____

Going Further How do you think temperature might affect transpiration?
How would you set up a test?

My Hypothesis Is:

_____

_____

My Experiment Is:

_____

_____

My Results Are:

_____

_____

Investigate Why Clouds Form

Hypothesize Sometimes the sky is full of clouds. Sometimes there are no clouds at all. Why? What makes a cloud form? What do evaporation and condensation have to do with it?

Write a **Hypothesis:**

_____

_____

_____

Watch what can happen when you cool off some air.

Materials

- hot tap water
- 3 ice cubes
- 2 identical clear containers
- food coloring
- mug
- refrigerator or freezer

Procedures

 Safety Be careful handling the hot water. Use the handle to hold the mug. Do not burn yourself.

1. Chill container 1 by putting it in a refrigerator or on ice for about ten minutes.

2. Fill a mug with hot tap water.

3. **Make a Model** Fill container 2 with hot water. Place empty cold container 1 upside down on top of container 2 with the water. Fit the mouths together carefully. Place the ice cubes on top of container 1.

4. **Observe** Write your observations on another sheet of paper.

Conclude and Apply

1. **Communicate** What did you observe?

_____

_____

2. **Communicate** Where did this take place?

_____

_____

3. Communicate Where did the water come from?

_____

_____

4. Infer Explain what made it happen.

_____

_____

_____

Go Further: Apply

5. Draw Conclusions Where would you expect to find more clouds—over the ocean or over a desert? Why?

_____

_____

_____

6. Infer Why don't all clouds look the same?

_____

❓ Inquiry

Think of your own questions that you might like to test. Do dry conditions affect clouds?

My Question Is:

_____

How I Can Test It:

_____

_____

My Results Are:

_____

_____

Name _____

Feel the Humidity

Hypothesize Why do you feel warmer on a high humidity day?

Write a **Hypothesis:**

_____

_____

Materials

- 2-in.-square piece of old cotton cloth
- thermometer
- $\frac{1}{2}$ c of cold water

- rubber band
- 1 c of warm water

Procedures

▨ **Safety** Be careful handling warm water.

1. **Observe** Record the air temperature.

_____

2. Put the thermometer in cold water. Add warm water slowly until water temperature matches air temperature.

3. Wrap cloth around bulb of thermometer. Gently hold it with a rubber band. Dampen cloth in the water.

4. **Observe** Wave thermometer gently in air. Record temperatures every 30 seconds for three minutes.

Time	Temperature
30 seconds	
1 minute	
1 minute, 30 seconds	
2 minutes	
2 minutes, 30 seconds	
3 minutes	

nclude and Apply

1. **Infer** What happened to temperature of wet cloth? How does cloth feel? Explain.

_____

_____

2. **Infer** Suppose you try this experiment on a day that is humid and on a day that is dry. Will you get the same results? Explain.

_____

_____

_____

_____

Going Further In a school track meet, would sweating cool the runners more on a humid day or on a dry day? Write and conduct an experiment.

My Hypothesis Is:

_____

_____

My Experiment Is:

_____

_____

My Results Are:

_____

_____

Investigate What Can Change Air Pressure

Hypothesize Air moves from one place to another because of differences in air pressure. What causes these differences? Make a model to test your ideas.

Write a **Hypothesis:**

_____

_____

Put the atmosphere in a jar to explore air pressure.

Materials

- plastic jar with hole in bottom
- plastic sandwich bag
- rubber band
- masking tape

Step 1

Plastic sandwich bag — Plastic jar

Rubber band

Plastic jar

Hole

Procedures

1. **Make a Model** Set up a jar-and-bag system as shown. Make sure the masking tape covers the hole in the jar. Have a partner place both hands on the jar and hold it firmly. Reach in and slowly pull up on the bottom of the bag. Describe what happens.

   _____

2. **Experiment** Pull the small piece of tape off the hole in the bottom of the jar. Repeat step 1. Push in on the bag. Record results.

   _____

3. **Observe** Place some small bits of paper on the table. Hold the jar close to the table. Point the hole toward the bits of paper. Pull up on the bag, and observe and record what happens.

   _____

4. **Experiment** Do just the opposite. Push the bag back into the jar, and observe. What happened?

   _____

Conclude and Apply

1. **Compare and Contrast** What differences did you observe with the hole taped and with the tape removed?

   _____

_____

_____

2. Infer Explain what happened each time you pushed the bag back into the jar. Why did it happen?

_____

_____

_____

3. Draw Conclusions How does this model show air pressure changes?

_____

_____

_____

Going Further: Problem Solving

4. Use Variables Will the model work the same with paper clips? Bits of cotton? Rubber pads? Make a prediction, and test it.

_____

_____

Inquiry

Think of your own questions that you might like to test. Does air temperature affect air pressure?

My Question Is:

_____

How I Can Test It:

_____

_____

My Results Are:

_____

Name _____

Using Numbers and Interpreting Data

A Weather Station Model

A weather station model shows the weather at one weather station. A station model includes temperature, cloud cover, air pressure, pressure tendency, wind speed, and wind direction. The circle is at the location of the station. The temperature may be recorded.

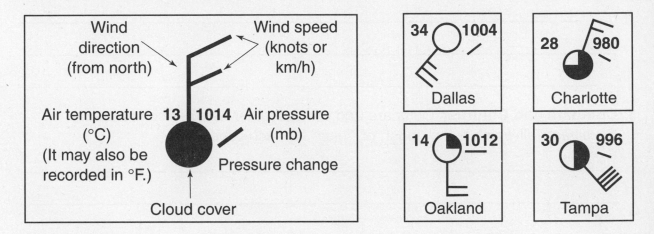

Procedures

1. **Use Numbers** Look carefully at the first weather station model. How fast is the wind blowing? What is the wind direction? Record your answers.

   _____

2. **Use Numbers** What other information does the first weather station model give you?

   _____

   _____

3. Look at the weather station models of the other cities. Make a table on the next page. In your table record the weather conditions for each city.

nclude and Apply

1. **Evaluate** Compare the information in the table you made with these station models. Which way is the information easier to interpret?

_____

2. **Compare and Contrast** Where was wind the fastest? The slowest? Which tells you this information more quickly, the chart or your models?

_____

_____

_____

3. **Compare and Contrast** Compare and contrast other weather conditions in the cities. Tell which is the "most" or "least" for each condition.

_____

_____

_____

_____

Investigate How to Compare Weather

Hypothesize How can you tell where the weather may change? Test your ideas. How would you use a weather map to give a weather report of the country?

Write a **Hypothesis:**

_____

_____

_____

Use a map and key to predict the weather.

Materials

- station model key
- pencil
- newspaper
- newspaper weather map (optional)
- crayons

Procedures

Communicate Think of the country in large regions—the Northeast, the Southwest, and so on. Think of regions like the Pacific Coast, the Atlantic Coast, and the Gulf Coast. Write a report for the weather in each region based on the map you see on page 55. Use another sheet of paper if necessary.

_____

_____

_____

_____

_____

_____

_____

_____

_____

_____

_____

_____

Conclude and Apply

1. Infer Which areas are having warm, rainy weather?

_____

2. Infer Where is the weather cool and dry?

_____

_____

Going Further: Problem Solving

3. Infer How do you think weather in any part of the country may change, based on the data in this map? Give reasons for your answer. How would you check your predictions?

_____

_____

_____

_____

4. Interpret Data Using weather maps in a newspaper or the one on page 148 of your textbook, describe the weather.

_____

_____

 Inquiry

Think of your own questions that you might like to test. Can temperatures vary within a small area?

My Question Is:

_____

_____

How I Can Test It:

_____

_____

My Results Are:

_____

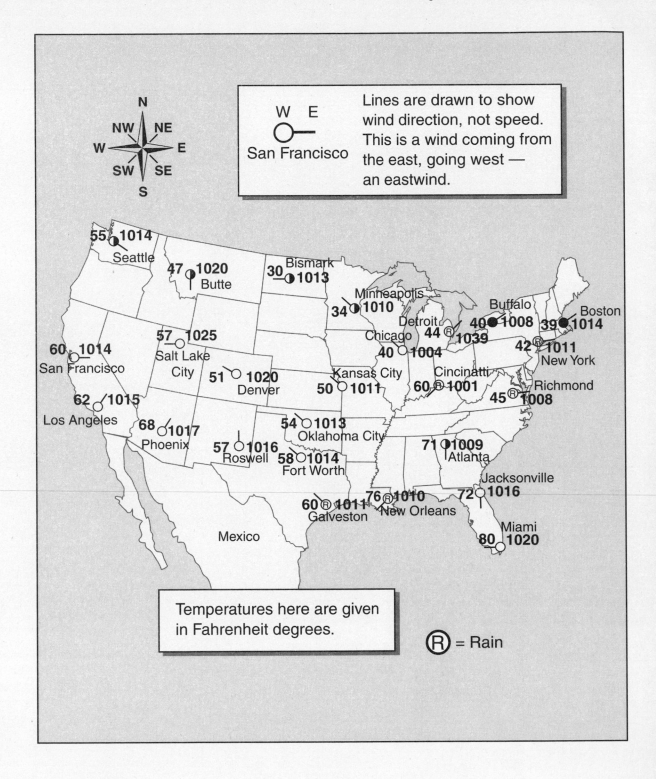

Lines are drawn to show wind direction, not speed. This is a wind coming from the east, going west — an eastwind.

W E
○——
San Francisco

Temperatures here are given in Fahrenheit degrees.

Ⓡ = Rain

Weather Prediction

Hypothesize How can you use a weather map to predict the weather?

Write a **Hypothesis:**

_____

_____

_____

Procedures

1. **Analyze** The map on page 65 shows weather in the United States at 6 P.M. on October 29. Describe the weather in Washington, D.C. The temperatures are in degrees Celsius.

_____

_____

2. **Analyze** Describe the weather in the northwest part of the country and the southeast.

_____

_____

_____

Conclude and Apply

Infer Weather patterns move from west to east across the United States. How do you think the weather in Washington, D.C., will change in the next day or so? Explain your answer.

_____

_____

_____

Going Further Why do you think forecasting the weather is important?

_____

_____

_____

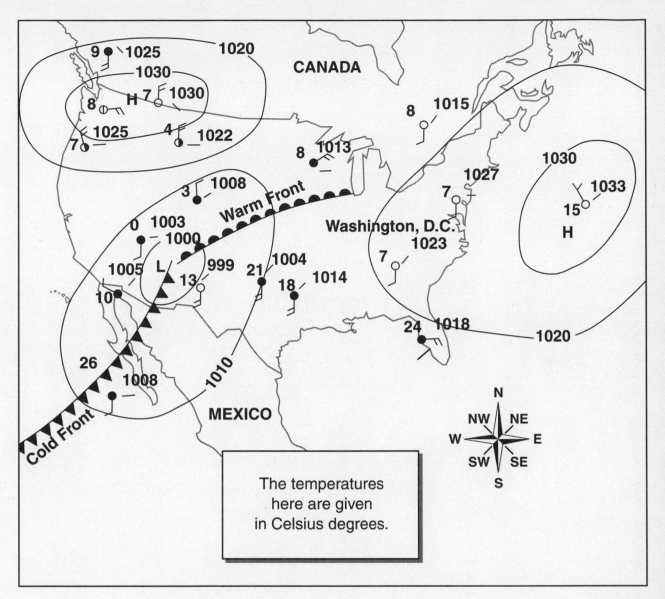

The temperatures here are given in Celsius degrees.

Investigate What Severe Storms Are

Hypothesize Tornadoes strike all parts of the United States. However, they are more frequent in some regions than in others. Where in the U.S. is "tornado country"? How might you test your hypothesis?

Write a **Hypothesis:**

_____

_____

To investigate what severe storms are, begin by plotting tornadoes on a map to tell where they are most likely to happen.

Materials

• blue marker   • red marker   • map of U.S., including Alaska and Hawaii, on page 71

State	Total	Average per Year	State	Total	Average per Year	State	Total	Average per Year	State	Total	Average per Year	State	Total	Average per Year
AL	668	22	HI	25	1	MA	89	3	NM	276	9	SD	864	29
AK	0	0	ID	80	3	MI	567	19	NY	169	6	TN	360	12
AZ	106	4	IL	798	27	MN	607	20	NC	435	15	TX	4,174	139
AR	596	20	IN	604	20	MS	775	26	ND	621	21	UT	58	2
CA	148	5	IA	1,079	36	MO	781	26	OH	463	15	VT	21	1
CO	781	26	KS	1,198	40	MT	175	6	OK	1,412	47	VA	188	6
CT	37	1	KY	296	10	NE	1,118	37	OR	34	1	WA	45	2
DE	31	1	LA	831	28	NV	41	1	PA	310	10	WV	69	2
FL	1,590	53	ME	50	2	NH	56	2	RI	7	0	WI	625	21
GA	615	21	MD	86	3	NJ	78	3	SC	307	10	WY	356	12

Procedures

1. **Infer** The table shown here lists how many tornadoes occurred in each state over a 30-year period. It also shows about how many tornadoes occur in each state each year. Look at the data in the table for two minutes. Now write what part of the country you think gets the most tornadoes.

   _____

   _____

2. **Collect Data** Use the red marker to record the number of tornadoes that occurred in each state over the 30-year period. Use the blue marker to record the average number of tornadoes that occurred in a year in each state.

Conclude and Apply

1. Use Numbers Which states had fewer than 10 tornadoes a year? Which states had more than 20 tornadoes a year?

_____

_____

_____

_____

2. Interpret Data Which six states had the most tornadoes during the 30-year period?

_____

3. Interpret Data Which part of the country had the most tornadoes?

_____

Going Further: Problem Solving

4. Draw Conclusions Many people refer to a certain part of the country as "Tornado Alley." Which part of the country do you think that is? Why do you think people call it that? What else might these states have in common? Describe how you would go about finding the answer to that question.

_____

_____

_____

_____

_____

? Inquiry

Think of your own questions that you might like to test. Do tornadoes in "Tornado Alley" occur most often during certain times of the year?

My Question Is:

_____

_____

How I Can Test It:

_____

_____

My Results Are:

_____

_____

Name _____

Name ___
Con
Ir

Tornado in a Bottle

Hypothesize How does a tornado form?

Write a **Hypothesis:**

_____

_____

_____

Materials

- two 2-L plastic bottles
- duct tape
- water
- paper towel
- pencil

Procedures

1. **Make a Model** Fill one bottle one-third full of water. Dry the neck of the bottle, and tape over the top. Use the pencil to poke a hole in the tape.

2. Place the other bottle upside down over the mouth of the first bottle. Tape the two bottles together.

3. **Observe** Hold the bottles by the necks so the one with the water is on top. Swirl them around while your partner gently squeezes on the empty bottle. Then place the bottles on a desk with the water bottle on top. Describe what you see.

_____

_____

clude and Apply

fer How is this like what happens when a tornado forms? Explain.

_____

_____

Going Further What kind of damage can tornadoes cause? Research newspaper articles and reference books to find out.

My Hypothesis Is:

_____

_____

My Experiment Is:

_____

_____

_____

My Results Are:

_____

_____

_____

_____

Investigate What Weather Patterns Tell You

Hypothesize What factors are used to describe the average weather pattern of a region? How might you use graphs of year-round weather in different places to test your ideas?

Write a **Hypothesis:**

_____

_____

_____

_____

Compare weather patterns in two cities.

Procedures

1. **Use Numbers** Look at the graph for city 1. The bottom is labeled with the months of the year. The left side is labeled with the temperature in degrees Celsius. Use this scale to read the temperature line. What is the average temperature in city 1 during July?

   _____

   _____

2. **Use Numbers** The right side of the graph is labeled with millimeters of precipitation. Use this scale when reading the precipitation bars. What is the average precipitation in city 1 during July?

   _____

   _____

3. Repeat steps 1 and 2 for city 2.

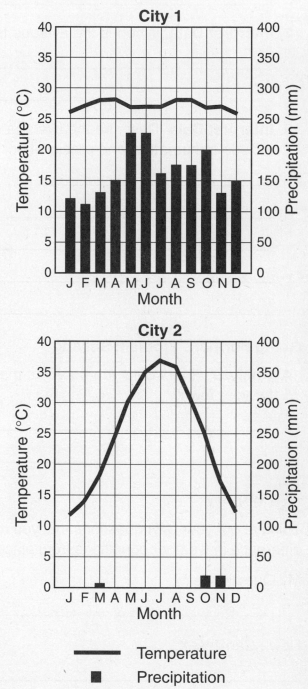

_____

Conclude and Apply

1. **Compare and Contrast** How do the annual amounts of precipitation compare for the two cities? Record your answer.

_____

2. **Interpret Data** When is the average temperature highest for each city? Lowest?

_____

_____

3. **Interpret Data** Describe the average weather pattern for each city. Be sure to include temperature and precipitation, and their relationship to the seasons.

_____

_____

_____

_____

_____

Going Further: Problem Solving

4. **Analyze** How would you go about making a graph of the weather patterns for your town?

_____

_____

 Inquiry

Think about your own questions that you might like to test. What causes the difference in weather conditions from place to place?

My Question Is:

_____

How I Can Test It:

_____

_____

My Results Are:

_____

_____

McGraw-Hill Science Unit: **WEATHER AND CLIMATE**

Making a Model

Climates in Two Areas

In this activity you will make a model of the soil conditions in the two cities described in Explore Activity 7. Use the information in the graph from the Explore Activity on page 85. The soil conditions you set up will model— or represent—the climates of the two cities.

Materials

- lamp
- spray bottle of water (like a plant mister)
- stick-on notepaper
- thermometer
- 2 trays of dry soil
- marking pencil or pen

Procedures

1. **Make a Model** Put 3 cm of dry soil into each tray. Label one tray City 1 and the other tray City 2.

2. **Use Numbers** What do the bars on each graph in the Explore Activity represent? Make a list of the amounts given by the bars for each month for each city.

	Precipitation (mm)			Precipitation (mm)	
Month	City 1	City 2	Month	City 1	City 2
January			July		
February			August		
March			September		
April			October		
May			November		
June			December		

3. **Use Variables** Model the yearly precipitation and temperature like this: Let 5 minutes equal 1 month. One squeeze of water sprayed on the tray equals 10 millimeters of precipitation. Every minute the lamp is on equals 20 degrees of temperature. That means that from 0 to 5 minutes is January. During January the City 2 tray gets no water and the lamp shines on it for $\frac{3}{4}$ minute. The City 1 tray gets 12 squeezes of water and the lamp shines on it for $1\frac{1}{4}$ minutes.

4. Model the two cities for all 12 months. Record your observations.

_____

_____

Month	Observations: City 1	Observations: City 2
January		
February		
March		
April		
May		
June		
July		
August		
September		
October		
November		
December		

Conclude and Apply

1. **Compare and Contrast** Examine the soil in the trays. Compare them at the same points in each year, for example, June and December. How do they differ?

_____

_____

2. **Evaluate** How does your model show climates?

_____

_____

Investigate What Makes Sound

Hypothesize What causes sound? Remember, sounds can be different. How could you build an instrument to test your ideas?

Write a **Hypothesis:**

_____

_____

_____

Test what makes sound by building a simple musical instrument.

Materials

- clear tape
- 30-cm (12-in.) wood or plastic ruler
- long rubber band (about 20 cm long before cutting)
- 210–270-mL (7-9-oz) plastic or foam cup

- ballpoint pen
- scissors
- goggles

Procedures

Safety Wear goggles.

1. Use a pen point to poke a hole in the bottom of the cup. Cut the rubber band. Insert one end into the hole. Tie two or three knots to keep the rubber band in place.

2. Tape the cup to the end of the ruler. Stretch the rubber band to the other end of the ruler. Tape it securely.

3. **Observe** Hold the cup next to your ear. Pluck the rubber band. Watch a partner do the same thing. Describe what you hear and see.

_____

_____

_____

4. **Experiment** Put one finger on the rubber band, hold it against the ruler, and then pluck it again. What happens to the sound?

_____

_____

© McGraw-Hill School Division

Conclude and Apply

1. **Draw Conclusions** What did you observe that made your instrument work? How can you explain what makes sound?

_____

_____

2. **Compare and Contrast** What happened to the sound when you changed the rubber band with your finger? Explain why based on your observations.

_____

_____

_____

Going Further: Problem Solving

3. **Predict/Experiment** What do you think will happen to the sound if you stretch the rubber band tighter? Untape the end of the rubber band and pull it a bit tighter. Retape the end to the ruler. Repeat steps 3 and 4. How do the results compare with your prediction? Give reasons for what happened.

_____

_____

_____

Inquiry

Think of your own questions that you might like to test. What other factors might affect sound?

My Question Is:

_____

_____

How I Can Test It:

_____

_____

My Results Are:

_____

Sound Carriers

Hypothesize Can sound travel through solids? Liquids?

Write a **Hypothesis:**

_____

_____

Materials

- sealable pint-sized plastic food bag filled with water
- wind-up clock
- wooden table or desk

Procedures

1. **Observe** Put the clock on the wooden table. Put your ear against the table. Listen to the ticking. Lift your head. How well can you hear the ticking now? Record your observation.

   _____

   _____

   _____

2. **Use Variables** Hold the water-filled bag against your ear. Hold the clock against the bag. How well can you hear the ticking? Move your ear away from the bag. How well can you hear the ticking?

   _____

   _____

   _____

Conclude and Apply

1. **Draw Conclusions** Rate wood, air, and water in order from best sound carrier to worst.

   _____

2. **Experiment** How would you test other materials, like sand?

   _____

   _____

Going Further Think of your own questions that you might like to test. Do some solids carry sound better than others?

My Question Is:

_____

_____

How I Can Test It:

_____

_____

_____

My Results Are:

_____

Design Your Own Experiment

How Can You Change a Sound?

Hypothesize Each musical instrument has a sound all its own. As you play an instrument, you make the sound change. What causes the sound to change? Test your hypothesis by building a homemade instrument from simple items like straws.

Write a **Hypothesis:**

_____

_____

Materials

- 12 plastic drinking straws
- metric ruler

- scissors
- masking tape

Procedures

1. **Predict** Work in pairs to make a homemade instrument. Try straws for starters. Blow over one end of a straw. Will there be a difference if you seal the other end with tape? Write a prediction.

_____

_____

2. **Observe** Tape one end and blow over the open end. Describe what you hear.

_____

_____

3. **Classify** Repeat with different lengths cut from a straw. Try at least four lengths. How are the sounds different? Arrange the straws in order to hear the difference.

_____

_____

_____

4. **Experiment** Flatten one end of a straw. Cut the end to a point. Wet it. With your lips stretched across your teeth, blow into that end of the straw. Try to make different sounds with the straw.

Name _____ EXPLORE ACTIVITY 2

How Can You Change a Sound? Page 2

Conclude and Apply

1. **Compare and Contrast** Why do you think the sounds changed when you cut different lengths of straw? Hint: What is inside the straw—even if it looks empty?

_____

_____

2. **Reproduce Results** Write a description of your instruments for a partner to build them exactly as you did. Include measurements taken with a ruler.

_____

_____

_____

Going Further: Problem Solving

3. **Experiment** Try other materials to make other instruments. Try such things as bottles with water, craft sticks, and so forth. Tell what causes the sound to change in each case.

_____

_____

_____

Inquiry

Think of your own questions that you might like to test. What other factors affect the sound an instrument makes?

My Question Is:

_____

_____

How I Can Test It:

_____

_____

My Results Are:

_____

_____

Skill: Communicating

Making Tables and Graphs

In this activity you will interpret data, classify sounds, and create your own table. Tables are helpful tools that organize information. The table shown gives the loudness of some common sounds in decibels (dB). Sounds below 30 dB can barely be heard. Quiet sounds are between 30 dB and 50 dB. Moderate sounds begin at 50 dB. At 70 dB, sounds are considered noisy. At 110 dB and above, sounds are unbearable.

LOUDNESS OF SOME SOUNDS	
Sound	**Loudness (in decibels)**
Hearing limit	0
Rustling leaves	10
Whisper	20
Nighttime noises in house	30
Soft radio	40
Classroom/office	50
Normal conversation	60
Inside car on highway	70
Busy city street	80
Subway	90
Siren (30 meters away)	100
Thunder	110
Pain threshold	**120**
Loud indoor rock concert	120
Jet plane (30 meters away)	140

Procedures

1. **Classify** Determine which sounds are barely audible (can barely be heard), quiet, moderate, noisy, or unbearable.

   Barely audible (can barely be heard) _____

   _____

   Quiet _____

   _____

Moderate _____

_____

Noisy _____

_____

Unbearable _____

_____

2. Communicate: Make a Table Make your own table to show how you
classified the sounds. Use another sheet of paper if needed.

3. Communicate: Make a Graph Make a data table to record how many quiet,
moderate, noisy, or unbearable sounds you hear in one hour. Make a graph to
show your results. "Number" is the vertical axis. "Kind of Sound" is the horizontal
axis. Put the data table and graph on a separate sheet of paper.

Conclude and Apply

1. Compare and Contrast How much louder is a soft radio than your house at
night? A classroom than a house at night?

_____

_____

2. Compare and Contrast How much softer is normal conversation than thunder?

_____

3. Communicate On another sheet of paper, make a chart listing loud sounds
in their environment. What you can do to protect your ears from harm done
by each loud noise?

_____

_____

Investigate If Sounds Bounce

Hypothesize What happens when sound "hits" a surface? Does the kind of surface make a difference? Test your ideas.

Write a **Hypothesis:**

_____

_____

Find out the effect different kinds of materials have on sound.

Materials

• 2 long cardboard tubes (can be taped, rolled-up newspapers)
• sound maker, such as a clicker or timer
• hard and soft test materials, such as book, wood block, cloth, metal sheet, sponge, towel

Procedures

1. Collect a variety of hard, smooth materials and soft, textured materials. Place one of the objects on a table. Set up your tubes in a V-shaped pattern on a table. The V should meet at the object you are testing. Record the name of the object in the first row of the table below.

2. **Observe/Compare** Place a sound maker (clicker or timer) at one end of the V. Listen for ticking at the other end of the V. Rank the loudness of the ticking on a scale of 1 (lowest) to 5 (highest). Record the number in the table.

3. **Experiment** Repeat steps 1 and 2 with the different materials you collected.

Material/Object	Loudness Ranking
1.	
2.	
3.	
4.	
5.	

Conclude and Apply

1. **Classify** What kinds of materials are the best reflectors—hard, smooth materials or soft, textured materials? What kinds of materials are the best absorbers?

   _____

   _____

2. **Make a Model** Draw a diagram of the path of sound from the sound maker to your ear. On your diagram mark the point in the path where the sound wave bounced.

Going Further: Apply

3. **Draw Conclusions** Theaters often have soft velvet curtains, thick carpets, and cushioned seats. How do you think these objects affect the sound in a theater?

   _____

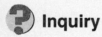 **Inquiry**

Think of your own questions that you might like to test. What other materials are good reflectors and absorbers?

My Question Is:

_____

How I Can Test It:

_____

_____

My Results Are:

_____

_____

Clap! Clap!

Hypothesize Can you cause a clear time lag between a sound and its echo?

Write a **Hypothesis:**

_____

_____

Materials

• meterstick

Procedures

1. **Observe** Stand about 8 meters away from a large wall, such as the side of your school building. Make sure there is plenty of open space between you and the wall. Clap your hands, and listen for an echo. Notice how much time there is between your clap and the echo.

   _____

   _____

2. **Observe** Move closer to the wall, and clap again. Listen for an echo.

   _____

3. **Repeat** Try this several times.

   _____

   _____

Conclude and Apply

1. **Observe** As you got closer to the wall, how did the time between the clap and the echo change? Did you always hear an echo? Explain.

_____

_____

_____

2. **Experiment** Repeat at different distances. What happens?

_____

_____

_____

Going Further Think of your own questions that you might like to test. Will you get the same results if you try other sounds?

My Question Is:

_____

How I Can Test It:

_____

_____

_____

My Results Are:

_____

_____

Investigate Whether You Can See if There Is No Light

Hypothesize Is it possible to see objects if there is no light? Test your ideas.

Write a **Hypothesis:**

_____

_____

Experiment with a shoe-box viewer.

Materials

- scissors
- flashlight
- small cardboard box with lid (a shoe box or a smaller box)
- small object to put inside box, such as an eraser, crayon, or coin (no sharp object)

Procedures

Safety Be careful using scissors. Do not put any sharp objects in the box.

1. Cut a hole about the size of a dime in the box as shown. Put an object inside the box and close the lid.

2. **Experiment** Look in the box through the hole. What do you see? Describe it.

_____

3. Now cut a small hole in the top of the box.

4. **Observe/Compare** Shine the flashlight through the top hole while you look into the box again. Can you see the object this time?

_____

Conclude and Apply

1. **Observe/Explain** Could you see the object inside the box in step 2? In step 4? Explain any difference in your answers.

_____

_____

_____

2. **Infer** Is it possible to see an object in the dark? Explain.

_____

_____

Going Further: Problem Solving

3. **Predict/Experiment** Do any characteristics of the object in the box affect the results? Try different kinds of objects. Predict any differences in your results. Test your ideas.

_____

_____

_____

_____

4. **Predict/Experiment** How much extra lighting would you need on a dark, cloudy day in order to safely walk around your room at home or your classroom? Would a night-light work? Would a lamp with a single light bulb work? How would you test your ideas safely?

_____

_____

_____

_____

 Inquiry

Think of your own questions that you might like to test. What other factors about objects in the box might make them visible?

My Question Is:

_____

How I Can Test It:

_____

My Results Are:

_____

Follow the Bouncing Light

Hypothesize How does light travel when it bounces off a mirror?

Write a **Hypothesis:**

_____

_____

Materials

• mirror
• string

Procedures

1. Sit close together. Hold the mirror as shown. Adjust it so your partner can see your face in the middle of the mirror.

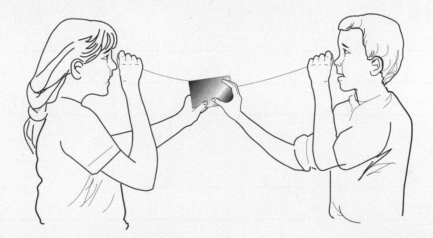

2. Have you and your partner hold a piece of string as shown. Note the angles formed between the string and the mirror.

3. **Observe** Move a little farther apart. Repeat the procedure. How does the mirror have to be moved in order for your partner to see your face? Try at several other positions.

_____

_____

_____

Conclude and Apply

Draw Conclusions

Were both of you able to see each other in the mirror? What did you observe
about the angles the string made with the mirror?

_____

_____

_____

Going Further Think of your own questions that you might like to test. Will light
bounce off objects other than mirrors?

My Question Is:

_____

How I Can Test It:

_____

_____

_____

My Results Are:

_____

_____

_____

Investigate What Light Can Pass Through

Hypothesize How do objects cast shadows? Do all objects cast shadows the same way? Are all shadows alike? How would you test your ideas?

Write a **Hypothesis:**

_____

_____

_____

Test materials to see if they all cast the same kind of shadows, if any at all.

Materials

- plastic sandwich bag
- clear plastic cup
- aluminum foil
- flashlight
- waxed paper
- food dye
- paper
- water (other liquids, optional)
- other assorted materials to test

Procedures

1. **Predict/Classify** Sort the test materials into those that you think light can pass through and those that light cannot pass through.

2. **Experiment** Use the flashlight to test if light can pass through each of the solid materials. Record your observations. Test if light will pass through water. What about water colored with food dye?

_____

_____

_____

_____

3. **Plan** How can you test if light passes through gases? Explain. What materials would you need?

_____

_____

Conclude and Apply

1. **Observe** Did all the materials allow light to pass through?

_____

2. Interpret Data Can light pass through all the materials equally well?

_____

3. Interpret Data Can light pass through solids, liquids, and gases?

_____

_____

Going Further: Problem Solving

4. Experiment Design a room in which shadows of objects are always soft and fuzzy, never sharp. What sorts of materials would you use?

_____

_____

_____

5. Predict/Experiment What else might you add to water to see if light gets through—sand, ink, instant coffee? Predict if each lets light through. How would you test your ideas?

_____

_____

_____

? Inquiry

Think of your own questions that you might like to test. What other factors affect shadows?

My Question Is:

_____

How I Can Test It:

_____

_____

My Results Are:

_____

_____

Seeing Through a Lens

Hypothesize What happens when you view the room through a lens? How does it change the way things look?

Write a **Hypothesis:**

_____

_____

Materials

• convex lens (magnifying glass)
• index card or piece of paper

Procedures

1. **Observe** Hold the lens about a foot from your eye. View the image of the room around you. Record what you see.

   _____

   _____

2. Repeat with the lens quite close to the page of a book.

   _____

   _____

3. **Experiment** Aim the lens at a light bulb or window. Move the index card back and forth on the other side of the lens until you see an image of the light source cast sharply on the card. Record what you see.

   _____

   _____

Conclude and Apply

1. **Observe** When the image was upright, was it enlarged or reduced?

   _____

2. **Observe/Compare** When you cast an image on the card, was it upright or inverted?

   _____

3. **Classify** Summarize your observations in a table on a separate sheet of paper.

Going Further Think of your own questions that you might like to test. Does the distance of the object from the lens affect the image?

My Question Is:

_____

_____

How I Can Test It:

_____

_____

My Results Are:

_____

Investigate What Color Is

Hypothesize What color will a blue object appear to be if you look at it under a blue light? Under a red light? How could you test your ideas even if you did not have a red or blue light bulb?

Write a **Hypothesis:**

_____

_____

Investigate how colored lights affect colors of objects by shining white light through different-colored cellophanes.

Materials

- red, yellow, blue, and green cellophane sheets
- red, yellow, blue, green, and black squares of construction paper
- white paper • crayons • flashlight

Procedures

1. **Observe** Shine a flashlight at a sheet of white paper through each of the cellophane sheets. Record what you see.

   _____

   _____

2. **Predict** What color will each of the colored squares appear to be through each of the cellophane sheets?

   _____

   _____

3. **Observe/Evaluate** After you have made your predictions, look at the colored squares through the cellophane sheets. Check your predictions.

   _____

   _____

4. **Make a Model** Use the crayons to make additional colored squares to view through the cellophane sheets.

5. **Communicate** Make a table on a separate sheet of paper that shows what color each square appears to be through each of the cellophane sheets.

Conclude and Apply

1. Communicate What color does the red square appear to be when viewed through the red cellophane sheet? Why?

_____

_____

_____

2. Communicate What color does the blue square appear to be when viewed through the red cellophane sheet? Why?

_____

_____

_____

Going Further: Problem Solving

3. Predict What do you think would happen if you looked at the red square through both the red and blue cellophane sheets at the same time? Try it to test your prediction.

_____

_____

_____

Inquiry

Think of your own questions that you might like to test. How does mixing colors of light differ from other ways to mix colors?

My Question Is:

_____

_____

How I Can Test It:

_____

_____

My Results Are:

_____

_____

Skill: Predicting and Observing

Materials

- red, yellow, blue and green food dyes
- water
- plastic cups
- goggles

Procedures

Safety Wear goggles.

1. Place four cups on a piece of paper. Add enough water to each cup to cover the bottom.

2. **Predict** What color will be made by mixing one drop of red food dye and one drop of yellow food dye in the water? Mix well. Describe the result.

	Red/Yellow
Prediction	
Results	

3. **Experiment** Do step 2 with red and blue dyes. Be sure to make a prediction before you mix the colors.

	Red/Blue
Prediction	
Results	

4. **Experiment** Do step 2 again with yellow and blue, and then with all four colors. Again, be sure to make your predictions before you mix the colors.

	Yellow/Blue
Prediction	
Results	

	Four Colors
Prediction	
Results	

Conclude and Apply

1. **Communicate** What color resulted when you mixed red and yellow? Why?

_____

_____

2. **Communicate** What color resulted when you mixed red and blue? Blue and yellow? When you mixed all four colors?

_____

_____

3. **Cause and Effect** What would happen if you used different amounts of each dye? Experiment to find out. Make predictions about the final color before you mix the dyes.

Color/Amount	Prediction	Results

McGraw-Hill Science Unit: THE ENERGY OF SOUND AND LIGHT

Investigate How Waves Move

Hypothesize How can you make waves move faster or slower? Test your ideas.

Write a **Hypothesis:**

_____

_____

_____

Build a wave to explore what makes waves move faster or slower.

Materials

- two 1-m strips of tape
- meterstick
- stopwatch or digital watch
- 20 straws
- 20 paper clips

Procedures

1. Work in groups of four. Starting 10 cm from one end, press 20 straws onto the sticky surface of a strip of tape. Be sure the straws are 4 cm apart, centered, and parallel. Secure them with the second strip.

2. **Observe** Have two members of your group each take one end of the model, so it spreads out lengthwise. Have a third person tap a straw at one end. Have the fourth person time how long the wave takes to travel across from one end of the model to the other. Record the time it takes.

   _____

   _____

3. **Experiment** Repeat step 2 several times, sometimes with the model tightly stretched, other times with it loosely stretched. Record your results in the table below.

Description of Model	Time

Conclude and Apply

1. **Observe** In what direction does the wave move? In what direction do the straws move?

_____

_____

2. **Draw Conclusions** How does holding it tighter or looser change how the wave moves?

_____

_____

Going Further: Problem Solving

3. **Experiment** Place paper clips at the ends of the first ten straws. Repeat steps 2 and 3 of the procedure. What happens? Try other combinations of paper clips. What happens? Record your results in the table below.

Paper-Clip Combination	Results

 Inquiry

Think of your own questions that you might like to test. Does the strength of the force affect the motion of a wave?

My Question Is:

_____

How I Can Test It:

_____

My Results Are:

_____

_____

Water Waves

Hypothesize How do water waves affect the motion of floating objects? Test your ideas.

Write your **Hypothesis:**

_____

_____

Materials

- aluminum foil
- shallow pan at least 8 x 11 in.
- water
- pencil

Procedures

1. Fill the tray half full of water. Fold small squares of foil (1 cm by 1 cm) into tiny "boats." Place several of these boats on the surface of the water.

2. At one end of the tray, make waves on the water's surface. Do this by moving your pencil horizontally up and down in the water.

3. **Predict** What do you think will happen to the boats after two minutes? After five minutes? Record your predictions.

_____

_____

Conclude and Apply

1. **Observe** What happened to the boats? How did they move? How far did they move? Were your predictions correct?

_____

_____

_____

2. **Experiment** What happens if you change how fast you make the waves? What happens if you change the number of boats you use?

_____

_____

Going Further Think of your own questions you might like to test. How do the waves produced by other objects move?

My Question Is:

_____

How I Can Test It:

_____

_____

_____

My Results Are:

_____

Design Your Own Experiment

Which Is More?

Hypothesize What properties do you use to compare things? Are there different ways something can be "more" than other things?

Write a **Hypothesis:**

_____

_____

Materials

- golf ball or wooden block
- blown-up balloon
- equal-pan balance
- box, such as a shoe box, big enough for the balloon to fit in
- ruler
- string
- pail of water

Procedures

1. **Observe** Look at the golf ball (or wooden block) and blown-up balloon. Which is "more"? Think of how one object could be "more." Which is "more" when you use a balance? Which is "more" when you put it in water and see how much the water level goes up?

   Record your observations.

   _____

   _____

2. **Plan** Use the equipment to verify one way that one object is more than another. Decide which of the three objects is "more" and which one is "less."

   _____

3. Repeat your measurements to verify your answer.

   _____

4. **Compare and Contrast** Now use different equipment to compare the two objects. Is the same object still "more?" Explain.

   _____

5. Repeat your measurements to verify your answer.

   _____

Conclude and Apply

1. **Communicate** Identify the equipment you used. Report your results.

_____

_____

_____

2. **Compare and Contrast** For each test, which object was more? In what way was it more than the other object?

_____

_____

_____

_____

Going Further: Problem Solving

3. **Experiment** What if you were given a large box of puffed oats and a small box of oatmeal? Which do you think would be more? Design an experiment to test your hypothesis. Tell what equipment you would use.

_____

_____

_____

_____

 Inquiry

Think of your own questions that you might test. How might you compare two objects that are similar in size?

My Question Is:

_____

How I Can Test It:

_____

My Results Are:

_____

Making a Model

How Metal Boats Float

You have probably seen how a metal object like a nail or a spoon sinks in water. However, huge ships made of similar metal float even when they carry large cargoes. How is this possible? In this activity, you will make a model of a metal boat. Experiment to see how boats are designed so that they can carry heavy cargo.

Materials

- household aluminum foil
- large paper clips
- pan of water

Procedures

1. **Make a Model** Make a boat out of a 10-cm by 10-cm (4-in. by 4-in.) piece of aluminum foil. Then float it on water.

2. **Predict** Write down what you think will happen when you place more and more matter in the space taken up by the boat. What steps should you follow to test your prediction? Be sure to use only the materials listed above.

   _____

   _____

3. **Experiment** Carry out your procedure, keeping a written record of what you observe.

   _____

   _____

   _____

   _____

   _____

Conclude and Apply

1. **Communicate** How well did your results agree with your prediction?

   _____

   _____

2. **Compare** Compare your model with those of your classmates. Which boat held the most clips? Why?

   _____

   _____

   _____

3. **Make a Model** The aluminum foil boat is a model of a steel ship. Use the way your boat floats to explain how a steel ship floats. Why was using a model of a large ship helpful?

   _____

   _____

   _____

4. **Infer** Think about objects that have more matter packed into the space they take up than water does. Based on your observations, will such objects sink or float in water? Design an experiment to test your prediction.

   _____

   _____

   _____

   _____

   _____

   _____

Investigate How We Know What's "Inside" Matter

Hypothesize How can you tell what is inside a sealed opaque box without opening it? What sorts of tests would you perform to try to identify its contents?

Write a **Hypothesis:**

_____

_____

You will examine three boxes to tell how one box has something in common with each of the other two.

Materials

• 3 identical, sealed, opaque boxes

Procedures

1. **Observe** Examine the three boxes, but do not open them. You can lift them, shake them, listen to the noises they make, feel the way their contents shift as you move them, and so on. Record your observations.

_____

_____

2. **Infer** Try to determine what is in each box.

_____

_____

Box	Observations	Object(s)
#1		
#2		
#3		

Conclude and Apply

1. Communicate Describe what you think is in each box.

_____

_____

2. How did you make your decision? _____

_____

3. Compare and Contrast Do these boxes have anything in common? In what ways

are they similar? In what ways are they different? _____

_____

_____

_____

Going Further: Problem Solving

4. Experiment What if you had a can of peanuts and a can of stewed tomatoes? The cans looked the same except for the labels. Now what if your baby brother took the labels off? You wanted the peanuts, but you didn't want to open the tomatoes by mistake. What experiments could you do to find out what was inside—before you opened a can?

_____

_____

 Inquiry

Think of your own questions that you might test. How might I tell the difference between a liquid and a gas?

My Question Is:

_____

How I Can Test It:

_____

My Results Are:

_____

Modeling Molecules

Hypothesize How do different elements combine to form molecules?

Write a **Hypothesis:**

_____

_____

_____

_____

Materials

• large and small marshmallows
• toothpicks

Procedures

1. Using small marshmallows for hydrogen atoms and large marshmallows for oxygen atoms, make two H_2 molecules and one O_2 molecule. Join the "atoms" with toothpicks.

2. Count the number of "atoms" of each type you have in your molecules. Record these numbers. Take this many more marshmallows and make as many water molecules as you can, using toothpicks to join the atoms.

_____

_____

Conclude and Apply

1. **Observe** How many water molecules did you make?

_____

2. **Infer** Why would real water molecules have properties different from real hydrogen and oxygen molecules?

_____

_____

Going Further Describe other examples of elements combining to form new compounds. Write and conduct an experiment.

My Hypothesis Is:

_____

_____

My Experiment Is:

_____

_____

_____

My Results Are:

_____

_____

Investigate What Happens When Ice Melts

Hypothesize How does the temperature change as a block of ice melts? Does it increase?

Write a **Hypothesis:**

_____

_____

Take temperature readings to see what happens as ice melts.

Materials

- ice cubes
- graduated cylinder
- thermometer
- water
- plastic or paper cup
- heat source (lamp or sunlight)
- watch or clock

Procedures

1. **Measure** Put ice cubes in the cup. Add 50 mL of water to the cup. Swirl the ice-and-water mixture together for 15 seconds.

2. **Measure** Place the thermometer in the cup. Wait 15 seconds. Then read the temperature. Record your observation.

   _____

3. **Measure** Put the cup under a heat source (lamp or sunlight). Take temperature readings every 3 minutes as the ice melts. What happens?

   _____

4. **Measure** After all the ice has melted, continue taking temperature readings every 3 minutes for another 15 minutes.

   _____

   _____

   _____

Time	Temperature (As Ice Melts)	Temperature (After Ice Melts)
3 minutes		
6 minutes		
9 minutes		
12 minutes		
15 minutes		

Conclude and Apply

1. Observe What happened to the temperature as the ice melted?

_____

2. Hypothesize Why do you think you got the results described in question 1?

_____

_____

3. Infer What does ice become when it melts?

_____

Going Further: Problem Solving

4. Predict What do you think would happen if you didn't add any water to the ice? What do you think will happen if you add more water to the ice? Design an experiment to test each of your predictions. What do you think happens as you freeze water? How would you design an experiment to test your prediction?

_____

_____

_____

_____

Inquiry

Think of your own questions that you might test. How might the intensity of heat affect melting ice?

My Question Is:

_____

_____

How I Can Test It:

_____

_____

My Results Are:

_____

Collapsing Bottles

Hypothesize How does heat affect an empty plastic bottle? How does cold affect it?

Write a **Hypothesis:**

_____

_____

Materials

• flexible plastic bottle with screw cap
• pails of hot and ice-cold water

Procedures

1. **Predict** What do you think will happen to the empty plastic bottle when it is warmed? What do you think will happen to it when it is cooled? Record your predictions.

_____

_____

2. With the cap off, hold the bottle for a minute or two in a pail of hot tap water. Then screw the cap on tightly while the bottle is still sitting in the hot water.

3. **Experiment** Now hold the bottle in a pail of ice water for a few minutes.

Conclude and Apply

1. **Communicate** Write down your observations of what happens next.

_____

_____

2. **Infer** Write out an explanation of why the bottle changed as it did. Be sure to use the idea of how molecules move at different temperatures.

_____

_____

_____

_____

Going Further Do gases also contract and expand with changing temperatures?
Write and conduct an experiment.

My Hypothesis Is:

_____

_____

My Experiment Is:

_____

_____

_____

_____

My Results Are:

_____

_____

_____

_____

_____

Design Your Own Experiment

How Can You Take Things Apart that Are Mixed Together?

Hypothesize How can you separate substances that are mixed together in a way that they keep their properties?

Write a **Hypothesis:**

_____

_____

Materials

- sample of substances mixed together
- toothpicks
- paper (coffee) filters
- water
- hand lens
- magnet
- 2 cups or beakers
- goggles

Procedures

▨▨▨ **Safety** Do not taste your sample.

1. **Observe** Examine the sample your teacher gives you. It is made of different substances. One of the substances is table salt. What else does it seem to be made of? Record your observations.

_____

_____

2. Design an experiment to separate the various ingredients in your sample.

_____

_____

3. Carry out your experiment.

Sample	Observations
Color	
Size	

Conclude and Apply

1. Infer How many parts or substances were mixed into your sample? How did you reach that conclusion?

_____

2. Explain You knew one substance was salt. What properties of salt might help you separate it from the rest? Could you separate salt first? Why or why not?

_____

_____

_____

3. Explain How did you separate out the substances? How did you use the properties of these substances to separate them?

_____

_____

_____

Going Further: Problem Solving

4. Experiment What if you were given white sand and sugar mixed together? How would you separate the two ingredients?

_____

_____

 Inquiry

Think of your own questions that you might test. What other senses might help you separate substances?

My Question Is:

_____

How I Can Test It:

_____

My Results Are:

_____

Kitchen Colloids

Hypothesize What happens to cream when you whip it?

Write a **Hypothesis:**

_____

_____

Materials

- whipping cream
- 2 bowls
- wire whisk
- ice

Procedures

1. Pour some whipping cream into a bowl. Set this bowl in a bed of ice in another bowl. Let the cream and bowl chill.

2. **Experiment** Use the whisk to whip the cream until it becomes a fluffy texture.

3. **Observe** Let the cream warm and continue beating it. Observe how it changes. Record your observations.

_____

_____

Conclude and Apply

1. **Define** What kind of colloid is the whipped cream from step 2?

_____

_____

2. **Interpret Data** What is it made of?

_____

_____

3. **Infer** In step 3 you made a colloid called a solid emulsion. What is this colloid commonly known as? What do you think it is made of?

_____

Going Further What other colloids can you find in the kitchen? What are they made of? Write and conduct an experiment.

My Hypothesis Is:

_____

_____

My Experiment Is:

_____

_____

My Results Are:

_____

_____

_____

Investigate How You Can Recognize a Change

Hypothesize How can you tell if a substance changes into something else? What signs would you look for?

Write a **Hypothesis:**

_____

_____

Experiment to find signs that a substance has changed.

Materials

- baking soda
- baking powder
- cornstarch
- salt
- iodine solution

- vinegar
- water
- 4 toothpicks
- wax paper
- 3 droppers

- 4 plastic spoons
- permanent marker
- 7 small cups
- goggles

Procedures

Safety Wear goggles.

1. Copy the grid below on wax paper with a marking pen. Using a spoon, put a pea-sized amount of cornstarch in each of the three boxes in the first row.

2. **Observe** Use a dropper to add five drops of water to the cornstarch in the first column. Stir with a toothpick. Record your observations.

_____

_____

3. **Experiment** Using a different dropper, add five drops of vinegar to the cornstarch in the second column. Stir with a new toothpick. Record your observations.

_____

4. **Observe** Use a third dropper to add five drops of iodine solution to the cornstarch in the third column. Record your observations. CAUTION: Iodine is poisonous and can stain.

_____

_____

5. Experiment Repeat steps 1–4 for baking powder, baking soda, and salt.

_____

_____

_____

_____

_____

Conclude and Apply

1. Infer In which boxes of the grid do you think substances changed into new substances? Explain your answers.

_____

_____

_____

2. Infer Your teacher will give you samples of two unknown powders. Use what you have learned to identify these powders. Report on your findings.

_____

_____

_____

_____

Going Further: Problem Solving

3. Experiment What if you were given a mixture of two of the powders? How might you use your grid to identify them? Describe how you would set up your experiment.

_____

_____

McGraw-Hill Science Unit: MATTER

? **Inquiry**

Think of your own questions that you might test. What evidence might show a liquid changing to a gas?

My Question Is:

_____

How I Can Test It:

_____

My Results Are:

_____

	Water	**Vinegar**	**Iodine solution**
Cornstarch			
Baking powder			
Baking soda			
Salt			

Experimenting

Preventing Rust

You've learned that steel forms rust when it is exposed to oxygen and moisture. Rusting can ruin metal objects such as tools, car bodies, and ship hulls. Can you find a way to stop or slow rusting? In this activity you will experiment to try to find the answer. In order to experiment, you need to do the following things. Form a hypothesis. Design a control. Carry out your experiment. Analyze and communicate your results.

Materials

• steel nails and sandpaper   • paper cups   • goggles   • dilute salt water

Procedures   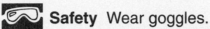 **Safety** Wear goggles.

1. **Hypothesize** You can make a steel nail rust by placing it in water. Think of a way to protect a steel nail from rusting under such conditions. Write an explanation of why you think your method will work.

   _____

   _____

2. **Experiment** To test your method of rust protection, you need a control nail kept under normal conditions. Each experimental nail will have just one condition (variable) change. For example, suppose you wanted to make a nail rust. You might leave one nail in a clean, empty jar (the control). You might put another in water. You might put a third in lemon juice. Write out how you will set up and control the nails for your experiment.

   _____

   _____

   _____

3. Experiment Carry out your experiment, and record your observations. Draw how the nails looked at the end of your experiment.

_____

_____

_____

Conclude and Apply

1. Infer Write out a description of how well your hypothesis agreed with your results. Be sure to compare the experimental nail to the control nail.

_____

_____

_____

2. Communicate Why did you need a control in this experiment?

_____

_____

_____

Investigate How Well Batteries Provide Energy

Hypothesize Is it better to buy heavy-duty batteries or less expensive ones? Which last longer? Which ones are really the least expensive to use?

Write a **Hypothesis:**

_____

_____

Test different batteries to see which is most economical.

Materials

For each circuit to be tested: • battery   • flashlight light bulb
                                   • 2 wires

Procedures

1. Connect one end of a wire to the light bulb. Connect the other end of the wire to the battery. Do the same for the other wire. Record what time the light bulb went on. Record the type, size, and brand of battery you used.

   _____

2. **Observe** Examine the light bulb every 15 minutes to see if it is still lit.

   _____

3. **Communicate** Record the time the light bulb goes off. _____

4. Repeat the experiment using another type or brand of battery.

   _____

   _____

Time	Observations
15 minutes	
30 minutes	
45 minutes	
1 hour	
1 hr. 15 min.	
1 hr. 30 min.	

Conclude and Apply

1. **Use Numbers** Divide the time each battery lasted by the cost of that type

   of battery. _____

2. **Compare** On another piece of paper, make a graph of the class's results.
   Which batteries lasted the longest? Which batteries cost the least per hour
   of use? Were some brands longer lasting? Were some brands cheaper to
   use than others? Were all batteries made of the same chemicals?

   _____

   _____

3. **Infer** Are the cheapest batteries the best buy? Are the longest lasting batteries the

   best buy? _____

   _____

   _____

Going Further: Problem Solving

4. **Apply** When might you choose the longest lasting batteries? The least
   expensive batteries? The bateries that cost the least per hour of use? Explain.

   _____

   _____

Inquiry

Think of your own questions that you might test. What other factors affect the cost
effectiveness of batteries?

My Question Is:

_____

How I Can Test It:

_____

_____

My Results Are:

_____

_____

Measuring Electricity

Hypothesize Can electricity affect a magnet? Can a magnet be used to measure electricity?

Write a **Hypothesis:**

_____

_____

Materials

- compass
- sandpaper

- 5 m of fine varnish-coated wire
- 1.5-V battery and bulb circuit

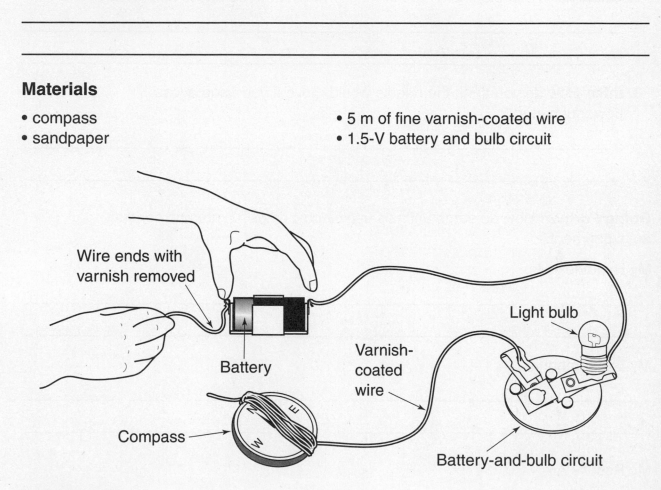

Wire ends with varnish removed

Battery

Compass

Varnish-coated wire

Light bulb

Battery-and-bulb circuit

Procedures

1. Wrap fine varnished wire around a compass. Use sandpaper to remove the coating from the ends of the wire.

2. Turn the compass until the needle is lined up with the coils of wire.

3. Keeping the compass this way, connect the ends of the wire to a circuit of a battery and small light bulb. See the diagram.

4. **Observe** What happens to the compass needle as you connect and disconnect the circuit? Record your observations.

_____

_____

Conclude and Apply

1. **Explain** How did you know when electricity was flowing in the circuit?

   _____

2. **Observe** When electricity was flowing, what did the compass needle do?

   _____

   _____

3. **Infer** How do you think the needle would move if you used a less powerful battery?

   _____

   _____

Going Further How do some animals use electric fields? Write and conduct an experiment.

My Hypothesis Is:

_____

_____

My Experiment Is:

_____

_____

My Results Are:

_____

_____

_____

Investigate How Earth and the Sun Are Held Together

Hypothesize How does a force hold Earth around the Sun? What would happen if the force let go?

Write a **Hypothesis:**

_____

_____

Use a model to explore the force between the Sun and Earth.

Materials

- clay
- scissors
- goggles
- 1 m of string
- meterstick

Procedures

Safety Wear goggles. Twirl the model close to the ground.

1. **Make a Model** Cut a 40-cm length of string. Wrap it around a small lump of clay in several directions. Tie the ends to make a tight knot. Measure 60 cm of string, and tie it to the string around the ball.

2. **Observe** Spin the ball of clay slowly—just fast enough to keep the string tight and keep the ball off the ground. Keep the ball close to the ground. Describe the path of the ball. Draw the path of the ball on another sheet of paper.

_____

3. **Experiment** At one point while spinning, let the string go. What happens? Describe the path of the ball of clay. Repeat until you get a clear picture of what happens.

_____

Conclude and Apply

1. **Describe** How did your model represent Earth and the Sun? What represented Earth? Where was the Sun located? How did you represent the force between them?

_____

_____

_____

2. Infer Explain what happened when you let the string go. Why do you think this happened?

_____

_____

_____

Going Further: Problem Solving

3. Use Variables How would your results change if the mass of the clay was doubled? Tripled? How does the mass affect the pull on the string? Make a prediction. Test it.

_____

_____

_____

 Inquiry

Think of your own questions that you might like to test. What other conditions affect the pull on the string or the path of the released ball of clay?

My Question Is:

_____

_____

How I Can Test It:

_____

_____

My Results Are:

_____

_____

Orbit Times

Hypothesize What does the length of time for an orbit depend on?
Test your ideas.

Write a **Hypothesis:**

_____

_____

Materials

• several sheets of graph paper

Procedures

Communicate Use graph paper. Draw a bar graph to compare the revolution
times for the planets. The vertical axis of the graph represents time. Decide
how much time each square on the paper represents. The horizontal axis
represents the planets. How many pieces of graph paper will you need?
Write your description.

_____

Conclude and Apply

1. **Draw Conclusions** Based on your graph and the data table, what
   relationship can you find between the length of the year (time) and the
   planet's location in the solar system?

   _____

   _____

2. **Revise** How could you change your graph to show the relationship even
   better? What might your new graph reveal?

   _____

   _____

   _____

   _____

Going Further Do all the planets travel at the same speed? Calculate each planet's speed. First calculate the distance traveled by treating the orbits as circular and calculating the circumference of the circle ($2\pi r$ where r is the distance to the Sun). Convert the orbit time from days to hours by multiplying the orbit time by 24 hours/day. Calculate speed dividing the distance traveled by the time in hours for a complete orbit around the Sun. Multiply the speed in million km/hour by 1,000 to report it in thousand km/hour.

PLANET	Distance Traveled (million km)	Orbit Time (hours)	Speed (thousand km/hour)
Mercury			
Venus			
Earth			
Mars			
Jupiter			
Saturn			
Uranus			
Neptune			
Pluto			

On a piece of graph paper, plot the average distance to the Sun versus the planet's orbital speed. What is the relationship between a planet's orbital speed and the distance from the Sun? Explain this relationship.

_____

_____

_____

_____

Design Your Own Experiment

What Makes the Crust Move?

Hypothesize What kind of motion causes an earthquake? Does it always cause destruction? Can it result in anything else? Test your ideas.

Write a **Hypothesis:**

_____

_____

_____

Materials

- 4–6 matching books (optional)
- layers of clay or modeling compound (optional)
- plastic knife (for use with clay)
- cubes
- wax paper

Procedures

1. **Make a Model** Work with a partner to use clay layers to model rock layers. You may use books, clay, or other materials to represent rock layers. Build your model on wax paper. Include a "crack" down through the layers. Stack cubes on the top of the model to represent buildings and other surface features.

2. **Experiment** Find as many ways of moving the model as you can to show how the crust may move during an earthquake. What happens to the surface features as you move the model each way? Describe each way you move the model. Draw the results on another sheet of paper.

_____

_____

_____

3. **Experiment** How can you show movement without causing any visible effect on the model buildings and other surface features?

_____

_____

_____

Conclude and Apply

1. Compare and Contrast How many different ways could you move your model? How were they different?

_____

_____

2. Cause and Effect Explain how each way you moved the model affected the surface features and changed the positions of the layers.

_____

_____

_____

_____

3. Cause and Effect How did you move the model without moving the surface features? Did the model change in any way? Explain.

_____

_____

Going Further: Problem Solving

4. Experiment How can you use your model to show how a mountain might rise up high above sea level? Explain and demonstrate.

_____

 Inquiry

Think of your own questions that you might like to test. What other effects can you demonstrate with the clay model? (Sometimes enough pressure is created when plates collide that part of a plate melts.)

My Question Is:

_____

How Can I Test It:

_____

_____

My Results Are:

_____

© McGraw-Hill School Division

Model of Earth

Hypothesize Can materials with different properties be used to make a solid Earth?

Write a **Hypothesis:**

_____

_____

Materials

- mashed ripe banana (in a plastic bag)
- peanut butter
- hazelnut
- graham cracker crumbs (in a plastic bag)
- wax paper

Procedures

Safety Students who are allergic to peanuts should not do this activity!

1. **Infer** You will use four materials to make a model of Earth on wax paper. Each material is one of Earth's layers. Read step 2. Decide which material represents which layer. Decide how thick each layer should be.

2. **Make a Model** Wash your hands. Cover the nut with a layer of peanut butter. Put the covered nut in the bag of mashed banana so that the banana covers it completely. Roll the result into the graham cracker crumbs on wax paper.

Conclude and Apply

1. **Draw Conclusions** Why does each material represent a different layer?

_____

_____

_____

_____

2. How thick did you decide to make each layer? Explain your reasoning.

_____

_____

_____

_____

Going Further Make a model of the plates in the Earth's crust. Mix dirt and water together to make mud. Pour the mud on to a cookie sheet. Place the cookie sheet in the sun for several days to dry the mud. When the mud is completely dry, press on the outer edges. What happened to the dry mud when you pressed on it? How can this be related to the Earth's crust?

_____

_____

_____

_____

Can you relate this model to the Earth's continents?

_____

_____

_____

Investigate How You Can Identify a Mineral

Hypothesize How do you think people can tell minerals apart?

Write a **Hypothesis:**

_____

_____

Compare properties of minerals to tell minerals apart.

Materials

- mineral samples
- clear tape
- red marker
- copper penny or wire
- streak plate
- porcelain tile
- hand lens
- mineral property table
- nail

Procedures

1. **Communicate** Use tape and a marker to label each sample with a number. On another sheet of paper, make a table with the column headings shown below. Use the table on the third page of this activity to help you identify your samples. Fill in the names of the minerals to match your samples.

Color = color of surface

Porcelain Plate Test = the color you see when you rub the sample gently on porcelain

Shiny Like a Metal = reflects light like a metal, such as aluminum foil or metal coins

Scratch (Hardness) = Does it scratch copper? A piece of glass?

Other: Is it very dense? (Is a small piece heavy?) Has it got flat surfaces?

Mineral	Name	Color	Shiny like a Metal (Yes/No)	Porcelain Plate Test	Scratch (Hardness)	Other
1.						
2.						

2. **Observe** Use the table shown as a guide to collect data on each sample. Fill in the table. Turn to the table on page 29 for more ideas to fill in "Other."

Conclude and Apply

1. **Analyze** Use your data and the table on the third page of this activity to identify your samples. Were you sure of all your samples? Explain.

_____

_____

_____

2. **Make Decisions** Which observations were most helpful? Explain.

_____

_____

Going Further: Problem Solving

3. **Draw Conclusions** How could you make a better scratch (hardness) test?

_____

_____

 Inquiry

Think of your own questions that you might like to test. Can minerals scratch each other?

My Question Is:

_____

How I Can Test It:

_____

_____

My Results Are:

_____

PROPERTIES OF MINERALS

Mineral	Color(s)	Luster (Shiny as Metals)	Porcelain Plate Test (Streak)	Cleavage (Number)	Hardness (Tools Scratched by)	Density (Compared with Water)
Gypsum	colorless, gray, white, brown	no	white	yes—1	2 (all five tools)	2.3
Quartz	colorless, various colors	no	none	no	7 (none)	2.6
Pyrite	brassy, yellow	yes	greenish black	no	6 (steel file, streak plate)	5.0
Calcite	colorless, white, pale blue	no	colorless, white	yes—3 (cubes)	3 (all but fingernail)	2.7
Galena	steel gray	yes	gray to black	yes—3 (cubes)	2.5 (all but fingernail)	7.5
Feldspar	gray, green yellow, white	no	colorless	yes—2	6 (steel file, streak plate)	2.5
Mica	colorless, silvery, black	no	white	yes—1 (thin sheets)	3 (all but fingernail)	3.0
Hornblende	green to black	no	gray to white	yes—2	5–6 (steel file, streak plate)	3.4
Bauxite	gray, red brown, white	no	gray	no	1–3 (all but fingernail)	2.0–2.5
Chalcopyrite	brassy to golden yellow	yes	greenish black	no	3.5–4 (glass, steel file, streak plate)	4.2
Hematite	black or red-brown	yes	red or red-brown	no	6 (steel file, streak plate)	5.3

Growing Crystals

Hypothesize How can you watch crystals grow?

Write a **Hypothesis:**

_____

_____

Materials

- foam cup half-filled with hot water
- granulated table salt
- 2 plastic spoons
- crystal of rock salt
- string (about 15 cm)
- pencil
- goggles

Procedures

Safety Wear goggles.

Your teacher will put a cup of hot water onto a counter for you.

Safety Use a kitchen mitt if you need to hold or move the cup. Do not touch the hot water.

1. Gradually add small amounts of salt to the water. Stir. Keep adding salt and stirring until no more will dissolve.

2. Tie one end of the string to a crystal of rock salt. Tie the other end to a pencil. Lay the pencil across the cup so that the crystal hangs in the hot salt water without touching the sides or bottom.

3. **Observe** Check the setup over several days. Record what you see.

_____

clude and Apply

Compare and Contrast Did any crystals grow? If so, did they have many shapes or just one? Explain your answer. If not, how would you change what you did if you tried again?

_____

_____

_____

Going Further Grow needle-shaped crystals. Dissolve Epsom salt in water. Line a shallow dish with black construction paper so the crystals will be more visible. Place a very small amount of the solution in the dish. Set the dish where it will not be disturbed. Check the dish after one day for long needle-shaped crystals.

Design Your Own Experiment

How Are Rocks Alike and Different?

Hypothesize Are rocks all alike? Are they different? If so, how?

Write a **Hypothesis:**

_____

Materials

- samples of rocks
- hand lens
- streak plate

- clear tape
- copper wire
- balance

- metric ruler
- red marker
- calculator

Procedures

1. Use the tape to number each sample in a group of rocks.

2. **Classify** Find a way to sort the group into smaller groups. Determine which properties you will use. Group the rocks that share one or more properties. Record your results.

_____

_____

_____

3. **Compare** You might consider hardness, the ability to resist scratches. Your fingernail, the copper wire, and the edge of a streak plate are tools you might use. Scratch gently.

_____

_____

_____

4. **Use Numbers** You might estimate the density of each sample. Use a balance to find the mass. Use a metric ruler to estimate the length, width, and height. **Length x width x height = volume; Density = mass ÷ volume**

_____

_____

Conclude and Apply

1. **Draw Conclusions** How were you able to make smaller groups? Give supporting details from the notes you recorded.

_____

_____

2. Analyze Could you find more than one way to sort rocks into groups? Give examples of how rocks from two different smaller groups may have a property in common.

_____

_____

3. Communicate Share your results with others. Compare your systems for sorting the rocks.

_____

Going Further: Problem Solving

4. Experiment If you could not easily measure your samples, how could you find their volume?

_____

_____

5. Infer How might some properties that you observed make a type of rock useful?

_____

Inquiry

Think of your own questions that you might like to test. How can you learn more about your rock samples?

My Question Is:

_____

_____

How Can I Test It:

_____

_____

My Results Are:

_____

_____

© McGraw-Hill School Division

Defining Terms Based on Observations

What Is Soil?

Earth's crust is made up of rocks and minerals. However, to get to the rocks, you usually have to dig through layers of soil.

Soil looks different at different places. It has different properties. Soil can be sandy. It can be moist.

Just what is soil? Make some observations. Write a definition that fits your observations.

Materials

- hand lens
- moist soil sample in a plastic bag
- 2 cups
- 2 plastic spoons
- sand sample in a plastic bag

Procedures

1. **Observe** Use a hand lens to examine a sample of moist soil. What materials can you find? How do their sizes compare? Write a description.

   _____

   _____

2. **Compare** Some soils are more like sand. How does a sample of sand compare with the moist soil sample?

   _____

3. **Use Variables** Which sample absorbs water more quickly? Fill a cup halfway with sand and another with moist soil. Pour a spoonful of water in each at the same time.

   _____

4. **Experiment** Which absorbs more water? Make a prediction. Find a way to test your prediction.

   _____

   _____

5. Experiment Make any other observations. Look for other differences.

_____

_____

Conclude and Apply

1. Draw Conclusions Based on your observations, what is soil make up of?

_____

_____

_____

2. Draw Conclusions How may soils differ?

_____

_____

_____

_____

_____

_____

3. Define Write a definition for soil. Take into account all your observations.

_____

_____

_____

Investigate What Makes Air Dirty

Hypothesize What kinds of pollutants are in the air that can make it look as it does in the picture on the opening page of Topic 5 of your textbook?

Write a **Hypothesis:**

_____

_____

_____

Try to collect pollutants to analyze them.

Materials

- 12 cardboard strips, about 12 cm long
- plastic knife
- string
- metric ruler

- petroleum jelly
- transparent tape
- hand lens
- marker

Procedures

1. Make square "frames" by taping together the corners of four cardboard strips. Make three frames, and label them A, B, and C. Tie a 30-cm string to a corner of each frame.

2. Stretch and attach three strips of tape across each frame, with all sticky sides facing the same way. Use a plastic knife to spread a thin coat of petroleum jelly across each sticky side.

3. **Predict** Hang the frames in different places to try to collect pollutants. Decide on places indoors or outdoors. Be sure to tell a parent or teacher where you hang the frames.

4. **Observe** Observe each frame over four days. On a separate page, record the weather, air condition (quality), and any change in the frames each day.

5. **Use Numbers** Then collect the frames. Observe the sticky sides with a hand lens and metric ruler to compare particles. Record your observations.

_____

_____

_____

_____

Conclude and Apply

1. **Interpret Data** How did the frames change over time? How did the hand lens and ruler help you describe the pollution?

_____

_____

_____

_____

2. **Communicate** Present your data in a graph to show differences in amounts. Use a separate piece of paper.

Going Further: Problem Solving

3. **Plan** What kinds of pollutants would your frames not collect? How might you design a collector for them?

_____

_____

4. **Plan** How might you extend this activity over different periods of time?

_____

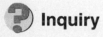 **Inquiry**

Think of other questions that you might like to test. What type of particles do common air filters trap?

My Question Is:

_____

_____

How I Can Test It:

_____

_____

My Results Are:

_____

Acids

Hypothesize How can acid rain change a rock?

Write a **Hypothesis:**

_____

_____

Materials

- chalk
- vinegar (a mild acid)
- goggles
- rubber bands

- limestone and other rock samples
- plastic cups
- plastic wrap
- plastic knife

Procedures

Safety Wear goggles.

1. **Use Variables** Break a stick of chalk into smaller pieces. Place some small pieces in a plastic cup. Place each rock sample in its own cup. Slowly pour vinegar in each cup to cover each object.

2. **Observe** Watch for any changes in the chalk and the rocks. Watch for several minutes and then at later times in the day. Record your observations.

_____

_____

_____

_____

3. Cover each cup using plastic wrap and a rubber band to help keep the vinegar from evaporating.

Conclude and Apply

1. **Explain** Vinegar is a mild acid. How did it change the chalk?

_____

_____

_____

2. **Compare and Contrast** Do all rocks change the same way?
   Explain based on your results.

_____

_____

Going Further Acid rain causes metals to deteriorate more rapidly. This can be
simulated using steel wool and vinegar. Write and conduct an experiment to
simulate more rapid deterioration of metal by acid rain.

My Hypothesis Is:

_____

_____

My Experiment Is:

_____

_____

_____

_____

_____

_____

My Results Are:

_____

Investigate How to Make Salt Water Usable

Hypothesize How can water with something dissolved in it be changed into fresh water? Test your ideas.

Write a **Hypothesis:**

_____

_____

Decide how the water cycle can make water fresh.

Materials

- tea bag
- plastic cup
- large, clear bowl or container
- deep pan
- saucer (or petri dish)
- water

Procedures

1. **Make a Model** Keep a tea bag in a cup of water until the water is orange.

2. **Make a Model** Place a pan where there is strong light (sunlight, if possible). Pour some tea water into the saucer. Put the saucer in the pan. Cover the saucer with a large bowl.

3. **Observe** Look at the bowl and pan several times during the day and the next day. Note any water you see on the bowl or in the pan. Write your observations.

_____

_____

_____

_____

Conclude and Apply

1. **Compare and Contrast** How was the water that collected on the bowl and in the pan different from the tea water?

_____

_____

2. Infer What do you think caused the water to collect in the bowl and pan?

_____

3. Draw Conclusions How does this model represent what might happen to salt water, the water of Earth's oceans?

_____

_____

_____

Going Further: Problem Solving

4. Use Variables How long did it take for water to collect in the bowl and pan? How might this process be speeded up?

_____

_____

5. Evaluate Do you think this model shows a useful way of turning ocean water into fresh water? Explain.

_____

_____

? Inquiry

Think of your own questions that you might like to test. What other substances can your model remove from water?

My Question Is:

_____

_____

How I Can Test It:

_____

_____

My Results Are:

_____

_____

Forming a Hypothesis

How Do Wastes from Land Get into Lakes and Rivers?

In seeking an answer to a question, the first thing you might do is find out as much information as possible. You make observations. You might look up information.

Next, you would think of an explanation for these observations. That explanation is a hypothesis. It may be stated as an "If . . . then" sentence. "If water runs over the land where garbage is dumped, then . . ." Sometimes you can test a hypothesis by making and observing a model.

Materials

- soil
- foam bits
- 1 L (2 c) of water
- food color
- 2 deep pie pans
- 2 textbooks

Procedures

1. **Form a Hypothesis** Write a hypothesis to answer the question above.

   _____

   _____

   _____

2. **Make a Model** Pack moist soil to fill one-half (one side) of the pie pan. As you pack the soil, add 10–20 drops of food color to the soil just below the surface. Sprinkle crumbled bits of foam over the top.

3. **Experiment** Use two books to tilt the pan with the soil side resting on the books. Place the lower edge of the soil-filled pan in the empty pan. Pour water over the soil in the uppermost edge of the pan. Describe what happens. Let your model stand for some time and observe it again.

   _____

   _____

   _____

   _____

Conclude and Apply

1. **Explain** How does this model represent wastes on land?

_____

_____

_____

_____

2. **Draw Conclusions** Based on the model, how do wastes from land get into water? Does the model support your hypothesis? Explain.

_____

_____

_____

_____

3. **Form a Hypothesis** How can wastes be removed from water? Form a hypothesis and test your ideas.

My Hypothesis Is:

_____

_____

My Procedure Is:

_____

_____

_____

_____

_____

My Results Are:

_____

_____

Investigate How People Use Energy

Hypothesize How many different ways do you use energy each day?
How can you use less energy? Test your ideas.

Write a **Hypothesis:**

_____

_____

Record all the ways that you use energy in a day.

Procedures

1. **Communicate** Make a list of all the different ways you use energy.
You might list cooking, heat or air conditioning, transportation, lighting,
entertainment (TV, radio, CD player), computer, and so on.

_____

_____

2. **Communicate** Make a list of all the different kinds of energy you use in a
day. Types of energy you might list include electricity (lights, TV, heat, air
conditioning), gasoline (riding in cars), gas (stove, heat), wood (fireplace), oil
(heat), and solar energy.

_____

_____

3. **Collect Data** Make a table listing all the kinds of energy you use in a day,
how you use that energy, and how many hours you use each. Put your table
on a separate sheet of paper.

Conclude and Apply

1. **Analyze** How many different ways do you use electricity each day? How
many hours a day do you use electricity? What other sources of energy do
you use? How many hours a day do you use each?

_____

_____

_____

_____

2. **Infer** Make a log to keep track of your energy use at home and at school. How can you use that information to help you make a plan to save energy?

_____

_____

_____

3. **Use Numbers** If it costs an average of ten cents an hour for energy you use, how much would the energy you use cost each week? About how much would it cost each month?

_____

_____

Going Further: Apply

4. **Hypothesize** How can you use less electricity? How much money do you think you could save on energy in a month? How would you go about testing your hypothesis?

_____

_____

_____

_____

 Inquiry

Think of your own questions that you might like to test. Making things uses energy. Can you conserve energy by throwing away fewer things?

My Question Is:

_____

How I Can Test It:

_____

My Results Are:

_____

_____

Fuel Supply

Hypothesize We are using fossil fuels at the rates shown in the table. How long will Earth's fossil fuel supply last?

Write a **Hypothesis:**

_____

_____

Procedures

1. Observe Examine the data in the table.

WORLD SUPPLY OF OIL AND NATURAL GAS (as of January 1, 1996)	
Oil	1,007 billion barrels (1,007,000,000,000)
Natural gas	4,900 trillion cubic feet
WORLD USE OF OIL AND NATURAL GAS FOR 1995	
Oil	about 70 million barrels a day (70,000,000)
Natural gas	about 78 trillion cubic feet

2. Communicate Draw a graph in the space below showing how long the fossil fuels we know about will last at our current rate of use.

Conclude and Apply

Infer Predict how long it will be until we run out of each type of fossil fuel.

_____

_____

Going Further Sources of energy other than fossil fuels are becoming more common. Write and conduct an experiment to learn about usage of alternative energy sources.

My Hypothesis Is:

_____

_____

My Experiment Is:

_____

_____

My Results Are:

_____

_____

Design Your Own Experiment

Hypothesize How do living things interact with each other and their environment? What do living things need in order to survive? How would you design a special environment to test your ideas?

Write a **Hypothesis:**

_____

_____

_____

What Do Living Things Need to Survive?

Materials

- wide-mouthed, clear 3.8-L (1-gal) container with lid
- pond water or aged tap water
- water plants such as *Elodea* or duckweed
- 2 large water snails or 8 small water snails
- grass seed and small plants
- 2 earthworms, 2 land snails, 4 sow bugs, or other small land animals that eat plants
- washed gravel
- soil
- small rocks

Procedures

1. For a water environment, add 4 cm (1.5 in.) of thoroughly washed sand or gravel to the jar. Fill the jar to about 4 cm (1.5 in.) from the top with water. Add a few floating plants, rooted plants with floating leaves, and submerged plants. Do not crowd the plants. Add two large or eight small water snails.

2. For a land environment, place a 2-cm (0.75-in.) layer of gravel on the bottom of the jar. Cover the gravel layer with a 5- to 7-cm (2- to 2.75-in.) layer of moistened soil. Add plants, and plant grass seeds. Add earthworms, sow bugs, and snails.

3. Place each jar in a lighted area but not in direct sunlight.

4. Cover each jar with its own lid or with a piece of plastic wrap. Record how many and what kinds of living things you used.

_____

_____

_____

5. Observe Examine your jars every other day. Record your observations on another sheet of paper.

Conclude and Apply

1. **Infer** What are the nonliving parts of your system? What are the living parts of your system?

   _____

   _____

2. **Infer** What do the living things need to survive? How do you know?

   _____

   _____

Going Further: Problem Solving

3. **Experiment** How could you design an environment that contains both land and water areas?

   _____

   _____

 Inquiry

Think of your own questions that you might like to test. How do changes in conditions in an environment affect the organisms in the environment?

My Question Is:

_____

_____

How I Can Test It:

_____

_____

My Results Are:

_____

_____

_____

Separating and Controlling Variables

Vanishing Bald Eagles

The chart below shows the average number of bald eagle eggs that hatched in the wild during a 16-year period. It also shows the level of an insecticide in bald eagle eggs during the same period. What is the relationship between these two variables?

BALD EAGLE EGG-HATCHING DATA																
Year	1966	1967	1968	1969	1970	1971	1972*	1973	1974	1975	1976	1977	1978	1979	1980	1981
Average number of young hatched (per nest)	1.28	0.75	0.87	0.82	0.50	0.55	0.60	0.70	0.60	0.81	0.90	0.93	0.91	0.98	1.02	1.27
Insecticide in eggs (parts per million) *pesticide banned	42	68	125	119	122	108	82	74	68	59	32	12	13	14	13	13

Variables are things that can change. In order to determine what caused the results of an experiment, you need to change one variable at a time. The variable that is changed is called the *independent variable.* A *dependent variable* is one that changes because of the independent variable.

Materials

• ruler

Procedures

1. **Infer** What is the independent variable in the study? What is the dependent variable in the study?

   _____

   _____

2. **Communicate** On a separate piece of paper, make a line graph showing the average number of young that hatched. Make another line graph showing the amount of insecticide in eggs.

Conclude and Apply

1. **Infer** Based on the graphs, what appears to be the relationship between the amount of insecticide in eggs and the number of young hatched?

_____

_____

_____

_____

2. **Hypothesize** Suggest a reason for the relationship.

_____

_____

_____

Investigate How Populations Interact

Hypothesize How can changes in a population lead to changes in the ecosystem it lives in? What kinds of changes might these be? How might you test your ideas?

Write a **Hypothesis:**

_____

_____

Use the cards to see what happens to a model ecosystem when changes occur in a population.

Materials

- tape
- string
- paper
- Population Card Resource Master

Procedures

1. Cut out the cards representing the plants and animals in the ecosystem.

2. Label the top of your paper *Sunlight.*

3. Place the plant cards on the paper, and link each to the sunlight with tape and string.

4. Link each plant-eating animal to a plant card. Link each meat-eating animal to its food source. Only two animals can be attached to a food source. Record the links on a separate piece of paper.

_____

_____

5. Fire destroys half the plants. Remove four plant cards. Rearrange the animal cards. Remove animal cards if more than two animals link to any one food source. Record the changes on a separate piece of paper.

Conclude and Apply

1. **Observe** What has happened to the plant eaters as a result of the fire? To the animal eaters?

_____

_____

2. Analyze Half of the plants that were lost in the fire grow back again. What happens to the animal populations?

_____

_____

3. Experiment Try adding or removing plant or animal cards. What happens to the rest of the populations?

_____

_____

Going Further: Apply

4. Drawing Conclusions If plants or prey become scarce, their predators may move to a new area. What will happen to the ecosystem the predators move into?

_____

_____

_____

Inquiry

Think of your own questions you might like to test. How would an ecosystem change if animals were removed from it?

My Question Is:

_____

_____

How I Can Test It:

_____

_____

My Results Are:

_____

_____

_____

Bison

Food: prairie plants

Prairie Plants

Food: made from water, carbon dioxide, and sunlight

Field Sparrow

Food: prairie plants

Prairie Plants

Food: made from water, carbon dioxide, and sunlight

Lizard

Food: insects

Prairie Plants

Food: made from water, carbon dioxide, and sunlight

Pronghorn Antelope

Food: prairie plants

Racer (snake)

Food: lizards, mice, insects

Meadowlark

Food: crickets, grasshoppers

Coyote

Food: rabbits, ground squirrels, meadow mice, other rodents

Prairie Plants

Food: made from water, carbon dioxide, and sunlight

Prairie Plants

Food: made from water, carbon dioxide, and sunlight

Bullsnake

Food: mice, rabbits, ground squirrels, birds and eggs

Field Cricket

Food: prairie plants, other insects

Ground Squirrel

Food: prairie plants

Red-Tailed Hawk

Food: ground squirrels, mice, rabbits, snakes, lizards, small birds

Badger

Food: ground squirrels, rabbits, mice, lizards

Prairie Plants

Food: made from water, carbon dioxide, and sunlight

Grasshopper

Food: prairie plants

Prairie Plants

Food: made from water, carbon dioxide, and sunlight

Cottontail Rabbit

Food: prairie plants

Prairie Plants

Food: made from water, carbon dioxide, and sunlight

Meadow Mouse

Food: prairie plants

Getting Food

Hypothesize What living things are in your community? Which are producers? Which are consumers?

Write a **Hypothesis:**

_____

_____

Materials

• Pencil

Procedures

1. Take a walk outdoors around your home or school. Choose a community to study. Make a list of the living things you see. Don't include people or domestic animals like dogs, cats, and farm animals.

   _____

   _____

   _____

   _____

2. **Classify** Organize the organisms into two groups—those that can make their own food (producers) and those that cannot (consumers).

Producers	Consumers

Conclude and Apply

1. Classify Which organisms did you list as producers?

_____

_____

2. Classify Which organisms did you list as consumers?

_____

_____

3. Communicate Draw two or more food chains to show how energy moves through this community. Use an extra sheet of paper if necessary.

Going Further How does the community you studied compare to other communities? Write and conduct an experiment.

My Hypothesis Is:

_____

_____

My Experiment Is:

_____

_____

My Results Are:

_____

_____

Investigate What Happens to Water

Hypothesize How can we, and all living things, keep using water every day and not use it all up? How would you experiment to test your ideas?

Write a **Hypothesis:**

_____

_____

_____

Use a model to see how water in the environment is recycled.

Materials

- plastic food container with clear cover
- small tray filled with dry soil
- 100-W lamp (if available)

- small bowl or cup filled with water
- 4-cm-square (1.6-in.-square) piece of paper towel

Procedures

1. Place the dry paper towel, the dry soil, and the bowl of water in the plastic container. Close the container with the lid.

2. **Observe** Place the container under a lamp or in direct sunlight. Observe every ten minutes for a class period. Record your observations.

_____

_____

3. **Repeat** Observe the container on the second day. Record your observations.

_____

_____

Conclude and Apply

1. **Compare and Contrast** What did you observe the first day? What did you observe the second day?

_____

_____

_____

2. Infer What was the source of the water? What was the source of the energy

that caused changes in the container? _____

_____

_____

Going Further: Apply

3. Draw Conclusions What happened to the water?

_____

_____

_____

4. Infer What parts of the water cycle does this model show?

_____

_____

_____

? Inquiry

Think of your own questions you might like to test. What happens to the salt in
ocean water when the water evaporates?

My Question Is:

_____

How I Can Test It:

_____

_____

_____

_____

_____

My Results Are:

_____

_____

Soil Sample

Hypothesize How do nutrients get recycled in nature?

Write a **Hypothesis:**

_____

_____

Test your hypothesis by examining a soil core.

Materials

• empty can

Procedures

Safety Do not touch the sharp edges of the can.

1. Go to a wooded area in a park or other location near your school. Find a patch of soft, moist soil.

2. Press a can, open side down, into the soil to get a core sample. You might have to gently rotate the can so it cuts into the soil.

3. Carefully remove the core so it stays in one piece.

4. **Observe** Describe the core and draw it on a separate sheet of paper.

_____

_____

_____

Conclude and Apply

1. **Infer** From the top to bottom, what kind of matter does the core hold?

_____

_____

2. **Infer** In what order did the layers form?

_____

_____

3. Infer Which layer holds the most available nutrients? Explain.

_____

_____

_____

Going Further How do worms help return nutrients to the soil? Write and conduct an experiment.

My Hypothesis Is:

_____

_____

My Experiment Is:

_____

_____

My Results Are:

_____

_____

Investigate What Controls the Growth of Populations

Hypothesize What kinds of things do organisms need in their environment in order to survive? What happens when these things are limited or unavailable? Test your ideas.

Write a **Hypothesis:**

_____

_____

Experiment to see how light and water can affect the growth and survival of seeds.

Materials

- 4 small, clean milk cartons with the tops removed
- 40 pinto bean seeds that have been soaked overnight
- soil
- water

Procedures

1. Label the cartons 1 to 4. Fill cartons 1 and 2 with dry potting soil. Fill cartons 3 and 4 with moistened potting soil. Fill the cartons to within 2 cm of the top.

2. Plant ten seeds in each carton, and cover the seeds with 0.5 cm of soil.

3. **Use Variables** Place cartons 1 and 3 in a well-lighted area. Place cartons 2 and 4 in a dark place. Label the cartons to show if they are wet or dry and in the light or in the dark.

4. **Observe** Examine the cartons each day for four days. Keep the soil moist in cartons 3 and 4. Record your observations.

_____

_____

5. **Compare** Observe the plants for two weeks after they sprout. Continue to keep the soil moist in cartons 3 and 4, and record your observations.

_____

_____

_____

Conclude and Apply

1. **Communicate** How many seeds sprouted in each carton?

_____

_____

2. **Observe** After two weeks how many plants in each carton were still living?

_____

_____

3. **Identify** What factor is needed for seeds to sprout? What is needed for bean plants to grow? What evidence do you have to support your answers?

_____

_____

_____

Going Further: Problem Solving

4. **Cause and Effect** Why did some seeds sprout and then die?

_____

_____

 Inquiry

Think of your own questions you might like to test. Do plants need anything other than water and sunlight to thrive?

My Question Is:

_____

How I Can Test It:

_____

_____

My Results Are:

_____

Playground Space

Hypothesize How much playground space does each student in your classroom have?

Write a **Hypothesis:**

_____

_____

Materials

- meterstick
- calculator

Procedures

1. Working in groups use a meterstick to measure the length and width of your playground.

2. Multiply the length by the width to find the area in square meters.

_____

3. Count the number of students in your class.

4. To find out how much space each student has, divide the area of the playground by the number of students.

_____

Conclude and Apply

1. **Infer** What would happen to the space each student had if the number of students doubled?

_____

2. **Infer** Assume two other classes with the same number of students as yours used the playground at the same time as your class. What effect might this have on your class?

_____

_____

_____

Going Further How many students can fit in your school? Write and conduct an experiment.

My Hypothesis Is:

_____

My Experiment Is:

_____

_____

My Results Are:

_____

Investigate Why Soil Is Important

Hypothesize Why is the soil in one kind of ecosystem different from the soil in another kind of ecosystem? What determines what the soil is like?

Write a **Hypothesis:**

_____

_____

_____

Test sand and soil samples to see which have the most nutrients.

Materials

- washed sand
- hydrogen peroxide
- 2 plastic spoons
- goggles

- compost, potting soil, or garden soil
- 2 plastic cups
- dropper
- apron

Procedures

Safety Wear goggles and an apron.

1. Place 1 tsp. of washed sand in a plastic cup.

2. **Observe** Using the dropper, add hydrogen peroxide to the sand, drop by drop. Count each drop. Bubbles will form as the hydrogen peroxide breaks down any decayed matter.

3. **Communicate** Record the number of drops you add until the bubbles stop forming.

_____

_____

4. **Experiment** Perform steps 1–3 using the compost or soil.

Conclude and Apply

1. **Compare and Contrast** Which sample—soil or sand—gave off the most bubbles?

_____

_____

2. Infer Why was the sand used?

_____

_____

_____

3. Infer Decayed materials in soil release their nutrients to form humus. The amount of humus in soil depends on the rate of decay and the rate at which plants absorb the nutrients. Which sample had the most humus?

_____

_____

Going Further: Apply

4. Evaluate In which sample could you grow larger, healthier plants? Why?

_____

_____

_____

_____

? Inquiry

Think of your own questions you might like to test? How much humus do other soil samples have?

My Question Is:

_____

How I Can Test It:

_____

_____

My Results Are:

_____

_____

Freshwater Communities

Hypothesize Do different organisms live in different locations in aquatic ecosystems?

Write a **Hypothesis:**

_____

_____

Materials

- dropper
- microscope slide
- coverslip
- microscope
- at least 3 samples of pond, lake, or stream water
- 3 or more plastic containers with lids

Procedures

1. Obtain samples of pond, lake, or stream water taken at different locations. CAUTION: Do not go beyond wading depth. Use a different container for each sample. Record the location each sample came from on the container.

2. **Observe** Place a drop of water on a slide, and carefully place the coverslip over it. Examine the slide under a microscope.

3. **Communicate** Record the location of each sample and what you see. Use low and high power.

_____

_____

_____

Conclude and Apply

Interpret Data What does this tell you about aquatic ecosystems?

_____

Going Further How do organisms in a different aquatic environment compare to those you examined in the activity? Design and conduct an experiment.

My Hypothesis Is:

_____

_____

_____

My Experiment Is:

_____

_____

_____

My Results Are:

_____

_____

Investigate How Ecosystems Change

Hypothesize Can different ecosystems affect each other when they change?
How might an abandoned farm and a nearby forest affect each other?
Test your ideas.

Write a **Hypothesis:**

_____

_____

_____

Compare what happened at Mount Saint
Helens to what might happen to an
abandoned farm at the edge of a forest.

Procedures

1. **Observe** Examine the drawing.

2. **Communicate** Describe the two
   ecosystems that you see.

   _____

   _____

   _____

   _____

   _____

Conclude and Apply

1. **Infer** How do the two ecosystems affect each other? _____

   _____

   _____

2. **Predict** If the land is not farmed for ten years, what would you expect the

   area to look like? _____

   _____

3. Draw Conclusions How can one ecosystem be changed into another?

_____

4. Compare and Contrast Read about Mount Saint Helens on pages 562 and 563 in the textbook. Compare what you think will happen to the abandoned farm with what happened at Mount Saint Helens. In what ways would the changes in the ecosystems be similar? In what ways would they be different?

_____

_____

_____

_____

Going Further: Apply

5. Analyze Think of another ecosystem that might be changed by nature. Think of another ecosystem that might be changed by humans. Describe how such ecosystems might continue to change over time.

_____

_____

_____

_____

? Inquiry

Think of your own questions you might like to test. How has another ecosystem been changed by nature?

My Question Is:

_____

How I Can Test It:

_____

My Results Are:

_____

_____

_____

Predicting Succession

Hypothesize In what areas where you live do you think ecological succession may be taking place?

Write a **Hypothesis:**

_____

_____

Procedures

1. **Observe** Identify an area near you where you think ecological succession is taking place.

_____

2. **Communicate** Describe the area. List the evidence you have that indicates ecological succession is taking place.

_____

_____

_____

_____

_____

_____

Conclude and Apply

1. **Infer** Do you think the succession will be primary or secondary? Explain.

_____

_____

_____

_____

_____

_____

2. Predict In what order do you think new species will colonize the area? Explain the reasons for your predictions.

_____

_____

_____

_____

3. Communicate Describe the climax community that you think will eventually live in the area. Give reasons for your conclusion.

_____

_____

_____

_____

_____

_____

Going Further Is ecological succession taking place in other areas near you? Write and conduct an experiment.

My Hypothesis Is:

_____

_____

My Experiment Is:

_____

_____

My Results Are:

_____

_____

_____

Interpreting Data and Inferring

Comparing Ecosystems in Volcanic Areas

In this activity you will collect and interpret data about the ecosystems of two volcanic areas.

Data are different kinds of facts. They might include observations, measurements, calculations, and other kinds of information. Scientists collect data about an event to better understand what caused it, what it will cause, and how it will affect other events.

What do these data tell the scientist? The scientist first organizes the data in some way—perhaps a table, chart, or graph. The scientist then studies the organized data and interprets it. *Interpret* means "draw a conclusion." In this case you will draw a conclusion about what determines which plants will return to a volcanic area.

Materials

• research books   • Internet

Procedures

1. Collect data on two volcanic areas, Mount Saint Helens and the Soufriere Hills volcano on the island of Montserrat or the active volcanoes of Hawaii. Organize the data on a separate sheet of paper.

2. **Communicate** Describe the sequence of events that has taken place.

   _____

   _____

   _____

   _____

   _____

3. **Interpret Data** Draw a conclusion about why certain plants return when they do.

   _____

   _____

   _____

   _____

   _____

   _____

Conclude and Apply

1. Compare In what ways is succession in the two areas alike? In what ways is it different?

_____

_____

_____

_____

2. Infer Why is the succession in these two areas similar or different?

_____

_____

_____

_____

_____

_____

3. Infer What abiotic factors must you consider when drawing conclusions? What biotic factors must you consider?

_____

_____

_____

_____

_____

_____

Investigate How Blood Travels

Hypothesize When blood is pumped by the heart, where does it go?

Write a **Hypothesis:**

_____

_____

Examine the path blood takes through your heart.

Materials

- sheet of paper
- tape
- 5 cm (2 in.) of red yarn
- 10 cm (4 in.) of red yarn
- two 10-cm pieces of black thread

- scissors
- four 5-cm-square white cards
- 5 cm of blue yarn
- 10 cm of blue yarn

Procedures

Safety Use the scissors carefully!

1. **Make a Model** Draw an oval about the size of your fist on the paper. Cut it out. Cut the oval down the middle and label it as shown.

2. Tape each piece of yarn to a white card. If *R* is the right side of the heart and *L* is the left side, trace the yarn and thread starting at *Out* on the *R* side. Sketch the model.

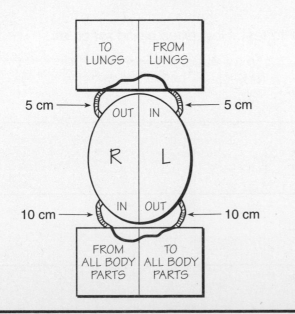

3. Compare Tape the halves of the oval "heart" together. Does the path of the yarn and thread change?

_____

Conclude and Apply

1. Sequence Assume blood flows through the yarn and the thread. Where does blood that enters the right side of the heart come from? Where does it go?

_____

_____

2. Compare and Contrast Where does blood come from to enter the left side of the heart? Where does it go? How is this different from the right side?

_____

_____

Going Further: Problem Solving

3. Draw Conclusions Why does the blood travel to the lungs? What do you think happens to the blood in the lungs?

_____

_____

_____

 Inquiry

Think of your own questions that you might like to test. How does blood reach all parts of the body?

My Question Is:

_____

How I Can Test It:

_____

My Results Are:

_____

Squeeze Play

Hypothesize How easy is it for your heart to pump blood? What might it depend on?

Write a **Hypothesis:**

_____

_____

_____

_____

Materials

- empty plastic water bottle
- masking tape
- pushpin

Procedures

1. **Observe** Squeeze the bottle with one hand, and feel how much air flows out with the other.

2. **Compare** Cover the opening with tape. Make a small hole in the tape with the pushpin. Squeeze. Does more or less air flow out? Is the bottle easier or harder to squeeze?

_____

_____

_____

Conclude and Apply

If your arteries start to narrow, will your heart work harder or less hard?

_____

_____

Going Further Demonstrate how the flow rate of water through a tube decreases when the tube diameter is decreased. Write and conduct an experiment. How does this experiment relate to the heart?

My Hypothesis Is:

_____

_____

My Experiment Is:

_____

_____

_____

_____

_____

_____

_____

_____

_____

_____

_____

My Results Are:

_____

_____

_____

_____

Investigate What Makes You Breathe

Hypothesize Many things can make it easier or harder for you to breathe. What might affect your breathing?

Write a **Hypothesis:**

_____

_____

Use this experiment to learn what forces help you to breathe.

Materials

- clear–plastic cup
- scissors
- small balloon
- 2 rubber bands
- flexible plastic straw
- pushpin
- large balloon
- clay

Procedures

Safety Use the scissors carefully!

1. Attach the opening of the small balloon to the end of the straw with a rubber band.

2. Make a hole in the bottom of the cup with the scissors or pushpin. Hold the cup upside down. Pull the open end of the straw through the hole so the balloon hangs inside the cup. Seal the cup hole around the straw with clay.

3. Tie the "neck" of the large balloon. Cut off the wide end. Stretch the balloon over the cup. Secure it with a rubber band.

4. **Observe** Pull down slowly on the stretched balloon. What happens to the small balloon inside the cup? Push up on the stretched balloon. What happens inside the cup? Record your answers.

_____

_____

_____

_____

Conclude and Apply

1. **Evaluate** Is there more or less space inside the cup system when you pull down on the large balloon?

_____

_____

2. **Identify** When you pull the large balloon down, what fills the extra space in the cup?

_____

_____

Going Further: Problem Solving

3. **Compare** How is the air pressure in the balloon similar to the air pressure in your lungs? Write down what you think happens when you breathe air into your lungs.

_____

_____

_____

_____

? Inquiry

Think of your own questions related to the breathing process. How does the expansion of the lung cavity change when you exercise?

My Question Is:

_____

How I Can Test It:

_____

_____

My Results Are:

_____

_____

Forming a Hypothesis and Measuring

How Exercise Affects Your Heart and Lungs

A hypothesis is a reasonable, testable guess or statement about why something happens. It helps you design and learn from experiments. If the hypothesis is correct, the results will support it. If the hypothesis is wrong, you must rewrite it.

Materials

• watch with a second hand

Procedures

1. **Hypothesize** Write a hypothesis about how exercise affects your pulse and breathing rates.

   _____

   _____

2. **Measure** Place your index and middle fingers on the inside of your partner's wrist so you feel a pulse, or beat, on the artery. Count pulse rate for one minute. Have another student count how many times your partner breathes during the minute. Record the number of heartbeats as the resting pulse rate. Record the number of breaths as the resting breath rate.

   _____

   _____

3. **Use Variables** Have your partner do jumping jacks for two minutes, then measure pulse and breathing rates for one minute. Record results.

   _____

   _____

4. **Compare** Wait two minutes, recount and record both results.

   _____

   _____

   _____

Conclude and Apply

1. Compare How much faster was the pulse rate after exercising? How much faster was the breathing rate?

_____

_____

2. Conclude How does exercise affect the heart and lungs?

_____

_____

_____

_____

_____

_____

_____

3. Revise Does this prove your hypothesis? If not, how can you change and test it?

_____

_____

_____

Design Your Own Experiment

What Are Some Ways to Sort Materials?

Hypothesize Every day your body uses some of the food you eat and turns some of it into waste. What does your body keep? How does it get rid of wastes?

Write a **Hypothesis:**

_____

_____

Materials

- tea bag
- ground pepper
- cloves
- plastic bowl
- spoon

- cup half-filled with water
- tea strainer or medium-sized strainer
- coffee filter
- scissors

Procedures

Safety Use the scissors carefully!

1. Cut open the tea bag. Pour the tea leaves into the cup of water. Add the pepper and cloves. Stir.

2. Open the coffee filter and hold it over the bowl. Hold the tea strainer above the open filter.

3. Slowly pour the contents of the cup through the strainer and into the filter.

4. **Observe** What is left in the strainer? What is left in the filter? Lift the filter. What is in the bowl? Record your observations.

_____

_____

Conclude and Apply

1. **Communicate** What was in the strainer at the end of the activity? What was not present in the bowl at all?

_____

_____

2. Explain Why did the filtering system work? Why can some materials pass through while others cannot?

_____

_____

Going Further: Problem Solving

3. Draw Conclusions How could your body use a system like this to separate solids from a liquid? Would this remove wastes effectively? Why or why not?

_____

_____

_____

_____

4. Experiment Design your own filtering experiment. Try placing different materials in different liquids, then filtering them out. Try other materials as filters. Answer **Conclude and Apply** questions 1 and 2 for your experiment. Record your results and conclusions on a separate page.

 Inquiry

Think of your own questions you might like to test. Gravity pulled the water through the filters in the experiment. Can liquids move through your body parts without the force of gravity?

My Question Is:

_____

How I Can Test It:

_____

_____

_____

_____

My Results Are:

_____

_____

Making a Model

How Your Kidneys Work

A simple way to understand how kidneys and nephrons work is to make a model. Models can help us understand how things work. You can use very simple materials and familiar objects to represent complex systems. This model will show the sorting process of your excretory system.

Materials

- plastic bag
- 5 red beans
- 5 white beans
- 5 rice grains
- 10 pennies

Procedures

1. **Make a Model** In this activity the bag stands for blood, the red beans for urea, the white beans for sugars, the rice for salts, and the pennies for water. Place the beans, rice, and pennies in the bag. What does the bag and its contents together represent?

   _____

   _____

   _____

2. Pour the contents of the bag on your desk to show materials moving from the blood to the nephrons.

3. Put all of the white beans back in the bag representing your blood. What does this illustrate?

   _____

   _____

   _____

4. Put four rice grains back in the bag to represent most of the salts.

5. Show that nearly all of the water returns to your blood by putting nine of the pennies back in the bag.

6. **Observe** Record what is left on your desk.

   _____

   _____

Conclude and Apply

1. **Explain** What items were left in step 6? What happens to these items in
   your body? What would happen if none of the materials in step 2 moved
   back into your blood?

   _____

   _____

   _____

   _____

   _____

   _____

2. **Predict** What would happen if none of the items ever left the blood?
   How could this harm your body?

   _____

   _____

   _____

   _____

   _____

Going Further: Apply

3. **Analyze** Many medicines are removed by your kidneys very quickly.
   How could you represent this in your model?

   _____

   _____

   _____

   _____

Investigate What Fitness Is

Hypothesize Being physically fit means your body is working at its best. Do you know what makes a body physically fit? How fit do you think your body is?

Write a **Hypothesis:**

_____

Explore skills needed for fitness.

Procedures

1. **Observe** Look at the pictures of the athletes on this page.

2. **Communicate** In each picture identify which body parts are being exercised. Describe what you think is the most important skill or ability needed to do each activity.

_____
_____
_____
_____
_____
_____
_____
_____
_____
_____
_____

Conclude and Apply

1. **Compare** How are the skills you identified different from each other? Are the skills different for each activity? Do some skills and abilities usually go together?

_____

_____

_____

2. **Evaluate** Everyone has certain skills and abilities. How do top athletes use their skills and abilities to succeed? What type of training is involved in different activities? How much time do you think top athletes spend each week practicing these skills? Why do you think most top athletes train for years in order to master their sport?

_____

_____

_____

Going Further: Problem Solving

3. **Analyze** Record some of your own skills and abilities. Think of activities that would help you use those skills.

_____

 Inquiry

Think of your own questions you might like to test. What skills and abilities are necessary for other sports?

My Question Is:

_____

How I Can Test It:

_____

_____

My Results Are:

_____

Hit the Target

Hypothesize Your heart rate indicates if you are exercising hard enough. How can you monitor your heart rate during exercise?

Write a **Hypothesis:**

_____

_____

Materials

• watch with a second hand

Procedures

1. To improve your heart and lungs, you must reach your target rate during exercise. To find your target rate, subtract your age from 220.

   _____

2. Multiply the result first by 0.7 and then by 0.8. Write the numbers down. Your target rate is between those two numbers.

   _____

   _____

3. **Compare** Take your pulse for one minute. Record the number. Take your pulse again after exercising for one minute. Record the new number.

   _____

4. **Draw Conclusions** How close is your heart rate after exercising to your target rate? Were you exercising hard enough to help your heart? Were you exercising long enough? How can your resting pulse tell you if your heart is getting stronger over time?

   _____

   _____

   _____

   _____

   _____

Going Further As your heart gets stronger do you have to work harder to maintain your target pulse rate during exercise? Write and conduct an experiment.

My Hypothesis Is:

_____

My Experiment Is:

_____

_____

_____

_____

My Results Are:

_____

_____

_____